China's Walled Cities

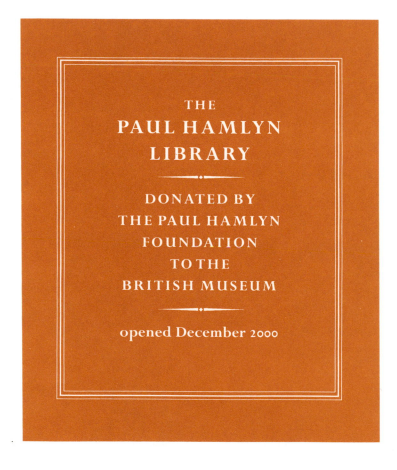

TITLES IN THE SERIES

At the Chinese Table
T. C. LAI

At the Japanese Table
RICHARD HOSKING

Arts of the Tang Court
PATRICA EICHENBAUM KARETZKY

The Birds of Java and Bali
DEREK HOLMES & STEPHEN NASH

China's Muslims
MICHAEL DILLON

China's Walled Cities
RONALD G. KNAPP

Chinese Almanacs
RICHARD J. SMITH

Chinese Bridges
RONALD G. KNAPP

Chinese Classical Furniture
GRACE WU BRUCE

The Chinese Garden
JOSEPH CHO WANG

The Chinese House
RONALD G. KNAPP

Chinese Jade
JOAN HARTMAN-GOLDSMITH

Chinese Maps
RICHARD J. SMITH

Chinese New Year
PATRICIA BJAALAND WELCH

Chinese Painting
T. C. LAI

Chinese Paper Offerings
RODERICK CAVE

Chinese Snuff Bottles
ROBERT KLEINER

Chinese Tomb Figurines
ANN PALUDAN

The Forbidden City
MAY HOLDSWORTH

The House in South-East Asia
JACQUES DUMARÇAY

Images of the Buddha in Thailand
DOROTHY H. FICKLE

Indonesian Batik
SYLVIA FRASER-LU

Japanese Cinema: An Introduction
DONALD RICHIE

The Japanese Kimono
HUGO MUNSTERBERG

Japanese Musical Instruments
HUGH DE FERRANTI

Korean Musical Instruments
KEITH HOWARD

Korean Painting
KEITH PRATT

Life in the Javanese Kraton
AART VAN BEEK

Macau
CÉSAR GUILLÉN-NUÑEZ

Mandarin Squares: Mandarins and their Insignia
VALERY M. GARRETT

The Ming Tombs
ANN PALUDAN

Modern Chinese Art
DAVID CLARKE

Musical Instruments of South-East Asia
ERIC TAYLOR

New Chinese Cinema
KWOK-KAN TAM &
WIMAL DISSANAYAKE

Old Bangkok
MICHAEL SMITHIES

Old Kyoto
JOHN LOWE

Old Manila
RAMÓN MA. ZARAGOZA

Old Penang
SARNIA HAYES HOYT

Old Shanghai
BETTY PEH-T'I WEI

Old Singapore
MAYA JAYAPAL

Peking Opera
COLIN MACKERRAS

Traditional Chinese Clothing
VALERY M. GARRETT

Series Editors, China Titles:
NIGEL CAMERON, SYLVIA FRASER-LU

China's Walled Cities

RONALD G. KNAPP

OXFORD
UNIVERSITY PRESS

OXFORD
UNIVERSITY PRESS

Oxford University Press is a department of the University of Oxford.
It furthers the University's objective of excellence in research, scholarship,
and education by publishing worldwide in

Oxford New York

Athens Auckland Bangkok Bogotá Buenos Aires Calcutta
Cape Town Chennai Dar es Salaam Delhi Florence Hong Kong Istanbul
Karachi Kuala Lumpur Madrid Melbourne Mexico City Mumbai
Nairobi Paris São Paulo Shanghai Singapore Taipei Tokyo Toronto Warsaw

with associated companies in Berlin Ibadan

Oxford is a registered trade mark of Oxford University Press

Published in the United States
by Oxford University Press Inc., New York

© Oxford University Press 2000

First published 2000
This impression (lowest digit)
1 3 5 7 9 10 8 6 4 2

British Library Cataloguing in Publication Data
available

Library of Congress Cataloging-in-Publication Data

Knapp, Ronald G., 1940–
China's walled cities / Ronald G. Knapp.
p. cm— (Images of Asia)
Includes bibliographical references and index.
ISBN 0-19-590605-5
1. City walls—China. 2. Cities and towns, Ancient—China. I. Title. II. Series.
NA497.C6 N36 2000
711'.4'0951—dc21

00-021817

Printed in Hong Kong
Published by Oxford University Press (China) Ltd
18th Floor, Warwick House East, Taikoo Place, 979 King's Road, Quarry Bay
Hong Kong

Contents

Acknowledgements   vi

1 Introduction   1

2 Chinese Wall-Building Traditions   3

3 Chang'an and Xi'an: Recalled Splendour   42

4 Beijing: Magnificent Imperial Capital   53

5 Nanjing: Forgotten Grandeur   77

6 Pingyao: Old China Preserved   87

7 Destruction and Preservation of a Legacy   98

   Selected Bibliography   105

   Index   109

Acknowledgements

NANCY SHATZMAN STEINHARDT and Joseph Cho Wang graciously read and commented on an early draft of this manuscript, and their critical comments are appreciated.

Illustrations were drawn from a variety of historical Chinese sources that are credited in the captions below the appropriate figure. In addition, some illustrations were drawn from books not included in the Selected Bibliography: Thomas Allom, *The Chinese Empire* (London: London Print. and Pub., 1870); L. C. Arlington and William Lewisohn, *In Search of Old Peking* (Peking: Henri Vetch, 1935); Wulf Diether Graf zu Castell, *Chinaflug* (Berlin: Atlantis-verlag, 1938); C. P. Fitzgerald, *China: A Short Cultural History* (London: Cresset Press, 1935); William Edgar Geil, *Eighteen Capitals of China* (Philadelphia: J. B. Lippincott Co., 1911); He Yeju, *Zhongguo gudai chengshi guihua shih* [A History of urban planning in China](Beijing: Zhongguo jianzhu gongye chubanshe, 1996); W.A.P. Martin, *The Siege in Peking* (New York: F. H. Revell, 1900); *Sketches of Nanking* (Nanking: Privately printed, 1933); John Stuart Thomson, *China Revolutionized* (Indianapolis: The Bobbs-Merrill Co., 1913); Wu Qingzhou, 'The Protection of China's Ancient Cities from Flood Damage' (*Disasters*, 13[3]: 193–227); Zhang Yuhuan, *Zhongguo gudai jianzhu jishu shi* [A History of Chinese architecture and technology](Beijing: Kexue chubanshe, 1985); and Zhu Ji, *Jinling guji mingsheng yingji* (Traces of old sites in Nanjing)(Shanghai: Commercial Press, 1936).

In addition to the contemporary photographs taken by the author, Nancy Shatzman Steinhardt and Joseph Cho Wang also each generously contributed a photograph from their collections.

1

Introduction

CONTEMPORARY CHINESE CITIES are usually encountered by the visitor as confounding mosaics of juxtaposed and competing landscape elements: post-modern hotels, imposing imperial gates, functional Stalinist-style apartment blocks, handsome Western-style banks, exquisite temple complexes, expansive squares, sublime gardens, broad tree-lined boulevards, flashy shopping areas, and dull neighbourhoods. Beneath this superficial jumble and half-hidden within the disorder of ongoing construction, it is sometimes possible to discern a quiet orderliness that whispers of a time when the structure of the city represented a cosmological scheme, an abstract idea given concrete shape and form. Few parts of a Chinese city's traditional plan were more expressive of this cosmology than were its walls. Encircling urban settlements, marking the outer contours of the symbols configured in the city's buildings and expressed in the site it occupied, it is these wrapping walls that are the subject of this book.

Walls indeed are a particularly Chinese preoccupation. Whether producing the high and blank outer walls that enclose a common courtyard dwelling or the imposing ramparts of the Great Wall, wall-building has a long history in China. As ubiquitous as is the use of walls to demarcate inner from outer, it is the association of walls with Chinese cities—the same word, *cheng*, is used for both—that permits one to elevate city walls to a significant architectural form and to treat them as more than mere functional fortifications. Throughout Chinese history, walled cities not only stood as outposts of imperial power in dangerous frontier areas, where walls served a protective purpose, but also served as symbols of imperial authority in core areas of the empire, where their function was clearly less defensive. Although constructed of massive yet ordinary materials, such as tamped earth and formed bricks, it was their majestic dimensions, as well as the embellished architecture of their gate and corner towers, that gave them grandeur. While able to serve practical needs, walls are also significant as visible and symbolic markers separating inside and outside, family and stranger. In short, they are as much visual dividers as psychological and symbolic markers.

Incomplete records in the imperial encyclopedia *Qinding gujin tushu jicheng* tell us that some 4,478 walls around large settlements had been built throughout the core eighteen provinces of China by the time of the Ming dynasty (1368–1644). Although the Ming was a period of great works of civil engineering, including wall-building, only 1,440 walled cities were still standing at the end of the dynasty as the Manchu conquerors began the Qing period (1644–1911). In the provinces of northern and north-western China with the longest history of wall-building, only a fraction of the city walls that had been built actually still stood during the seventeenth century, while in southern China, although there were fewer walls overall, far more of them remained at the outset of Qing rule. City, town, and village walls continued to be maintained and even some new ones built well into the nineteenth and twentieth centuries in response to the continuing tumult of civil disorder and warfare. Yet, the disintegration of the imperial system and the weakness of the government during the Republican period (1912–49) were both accompanied by the decay and demolition of city walls. More recently, over the past fifty years many historic walls have been deliberately dismantled. In the present day, intriguing remnants of China's old city walls remain, whispering of a time when no imperial city was complete without its signature enclosing structure.

2

Chinese Wall-Building Traditions

WALLS OF ALL TYPES have been conspicuous and meaningful components of China's cultural landscapes throughout the nation's history, but the form in which they appear has differed from period to period and region to region. Although agriculture has always been important, China's urban development is ancient in origin, extensive in scope, and brilliant in execution. Throughout dynastic history, China's urban areas have shared many common features related to site selection, construction materials and techniques, as well as their overall form. This persistence of external and internal form, as well as intrinsic structure—morphological elements—can be related in many cases to symbolic patterns or cosmological elements. A key to understanding any Chinese city is to examine the nature of its signature walls.

Site Preferences

Settlements come into being at specific locations for a host of reasons, but it is usually possible to determine the principal reason or reasons for a particular town or city to thrive while others fail. A panoramic survey at broad scale of the distribution of walled cities at any period in Chinese history provides a credible marker of the extent of imperial control at that time. A closer view portrays the specific site preferences and raises questions concerning the choice of city sites and the relation of the site to the surrounding hinterland. The key to understanding these relationships begins with the recognition that throughout most of Chinese history walled cities were sited in lowland areas. This condition contrasts markedly with European, Middle Eastern, and many Japanese cities that were perched upon prominent sites from which defenders would have a commanding military advantage. No such preference for an elevated, easily defensible site, however, seems to have nourished city site selection in China. Almost never was an elevated site chosen in northern China, and it is difficult even to find an upland city in the rugged south where promontories are common.

River banks have always been the preferred sites for Chinese cities. Transport, water supply, and, to some degree, security were facilitated by locating cities along a stream bank. Where river aprons were extensive, sites were chosen which allowed for ease of access to the river, and the shape of the walls could be quite regular. Where well-drained and flat sites were more restricted, the city's external form usually adjusted to whatever natural irregularity was presented to it, with the result that the shape of traditional Chinese cities sometimes includes wavy-sided walls.

Cities sited on the north bank of a river far outnumber those built on the southern bank, a situation that arises for a number of reasons. Chang (1977, 87) notes, 'As the frontiers of Chinese civilization moved first to the Huai and the Han, then to the Yangtze, and finally to the West River walled cities were in most cases built on the north banks, partly because land to the north would have been developed first by Chinese colonists and partly because the river could thereby provide a defensive barrier against the hostile or at least unfamiliar non-Han peoples farther south.' In addition, gently sloping hills on the northern sides of streams afforded better air circulation during summer and invited sunshine throughout the winter as well. It is thus no accident then that far more Chinese cities incorporate in their name the character *yang*, indicating 'the sun' and 'north of a river' or 'south of a hill', than include the complementary *yin*, with its opposite connotations.

Riverine locations often were prone to flooding and poor drainage. With their gates closed and banked with earth, the surrounding high walls provided a first level of protection against the menace of water (Fig. 2.1). Besides the walls themselves, however, it was not uncommon for cities to be protected by subsidiary embankments of earth, in the form of levees at some distance from the walls, as an additional precaution. In northern Jiangsu province in the eighteenth century, for example, the city of Huai'an was wrapped with a set of triple walls as a flood deterrent, because the city itself lay lower than the surrounding streams and walls. Drainage systems, in the case of Quanzhou, in Fujian province, included moats and canals that coursed through

2.1 Built adjacent to the Gan River during the Northern Song dynasty (*c.* 1069), the walls around the city of Ganzhou, Jiangxi province, served as a critical embankment to protect the city against floods.

the walled city in order to discharge the voluminous rains that fell on the region in the summer months (Fig. 2.2).

In certain areas of northern China where wind and sand storms are frequent, city walls served as screens against the ravages of cold winds and as a guard against the sweeping in of accumulations of sand. The steady north and north-west winds of fall and winter associated with the Siberian high pressure system often carry quantities of sand that pile up against the faces of north and north-west city walls. Western observers in the nineteenth century noted that sand and silt often amassed along the north wall of Kaifeng, in Henan province, to the degree that residents could enter the city by mounting the sweeping dunes that stretched to the top of the 7.5 metre high wall. The government earmarked specific funds in its annual budget for the periodic removal of this wind-blown accumulation.

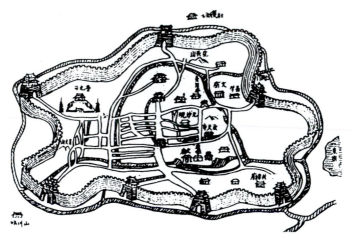

2.2 Ringed with a moat and linked to a river, the serpentine walls around Quanzhou, Fujian province, are pierced by a canal network that facilitates transport as well as draining rainwater. *Quanzhou fuzhi, c.* eighteenth century, after Wu 1989.

This preference for lowland areas is grounded also in the fact that Chinese generally did not perceive a striking dichotomy between urban and rural areas. For the most part, Chinese cities and towns, in early times and in recent centuries, did not develop for commercial or religious reasons—as was true of Western towns and cities—but rather sprang from bureaucratic decisions. Most came into being as the result of an imperial decision to create an administrative centre to express imperial control of an area. In this way, the walled city was one of the manifold legs propping up the empire: providing a steady flow of taxes and services to the court, as well as ensuring peace and security in the local area that made this largesse possible. Each walled city was foremost a visible manifestation of imperial authority and power, and each was inextricably linked to other walled urban units higher and lower in the administrative hierarchy. The remarkable uniformity in the layout and structures of Chinese cities is a reflection of their origins in a common set of imperial decisions, rather than the spontaneous and incremental growth patterns so characteristic of American and European cities and towns.

Figure 2.3 demonstrates the articulated relationship between a walled city and its hinterland, delineated by encircling mountain ranges. This diagrammatic map portrays the centrality of a walled administrative unit, surrounded by an area that faces inwards towards the city. The government itself was located within the city walls, but it administered the area within as well as outside the walls simultaneously and not separately. This relationship between the centre and the periphery is as much a representation of political reality as of economic and social interaction, and it can be seen at different scales, from that of the capital of the vast empire to an individual county. Wherever a walled city was located, it was not seen as a

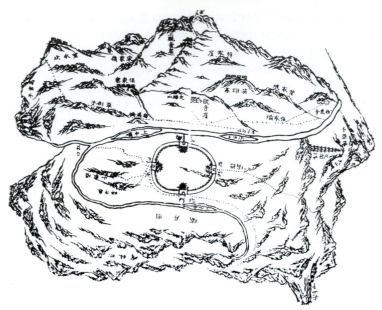

2.3 The centrality of a walled city within its well-defined hinterland is demonstrated in this characteristic Chinese map. Sited in the broad open expanse between the bends of a river, Xuanhan Xian, Sichuan province, the focal point for a region whose peaks and passes provide a first level of defence. Pang Lingping, *Xuanhan xianzhi*, Vol. 1, 1931.

solitary defensive unit detached from its hinterland.

In a general sense, the defence of an area was vested in the city's officials who, as surrogates of the emperor, secured the area's protection along its periphery rather than simply within the walls of the administrative city at its core. Guard posts and isolated forts perched on the ringing ridges helped to provide this kind of perimeter defence. In turbulent times, when defence of the periphery proved difficult, the rural population could retreat into the walled city. Chinese history is replete with descriptions of sieges of solitary walled cities, evidence of the regular failure of perimeter defence. Once peace was restored, rural folk would return to their lands and pick up their lives.

While the location of a walled city on an open plain, rather than on an elevated site, might appear to dismiss attentiveness to defensibility, attention was always given to nearby hills, passes, and streams within an area under official jurisdiction, because their control might be critical during times of turmoil. In sum, the city wall did not cleave either a physical or practical dichotomy between the urban and the rural. While the wall stood as an apparent massive physical barrier between the city inside and the countryside outside, its gates marked the psychological knots that tied together the city and the open area beyond.

Fengshui *and the Siting of Chinese Walled Cities*

It has sometimes been asserted that *fengshui*, Chinese geomancy, played a dominant role in both the site selection of, as well as the external and internal forms taken by, Chinese walled cities. Such assertions were especially common on the part of nineteenth-century observers, but some twentieth-century scholars have also found credible the notion that *fengshui* was a determinative factor in urban planning in traditional China. While the complexity of *fengshui* theory and practice is beyond the scope of this small book, it is useful to explore the topic briefly here in terms of the construction of China's walled cities.

General *fengshui* axioms, it is generally acknowledged, are based on notions that certain locations are more favourable than others and that, if such locations are identified accurately, then benefits will redound to those living in the selected places. Since places exist at different scales, some believe that by extension *fengshui* could plausibly be said to operate at all scales. *Fengshui*, which I have called elsewhere 'mystical ecology', centres most commonly on purposeful attempts to harmonize the residences of the living (houses) and those of the dead (graves) with their immediate physical environments. There is substantial evidence of the application of *fengshui* in choosing building sites, and in later making site adjustments for dwellings, tombs, temples, pagodas, and even whole villages, but there is a virtual absence of concrete details about the comprehensive application of *fengshui* to actual walled cities.

Xu Yinong (1996, 274), in his study of Chinese urban history and the development of Suzhou, concludes that one 'should be cautious not to over-stretch the evidence'. He suggests that 'the chief mode of [*fengshui*'s] application is characterized, not by actual practice in the physical construction of the city, but by interpretations involving diverse aspects of the city, ranging from its geographical location and natural setting to its form, space and individual structures.' Xu has masterfully documented that much of the *fengshui*-related activity regarding the walled city of Suzhou was retrospective, as he calls it, comprised simply of later attempts to manipulate structures and space for specific purposes rather than anticipatory planning of a consistent nature. Xu is vigilant in avoiding over-hasty generalizations, allowing that *fengshui* may well have been applied systematically to the building of some imperial capitals, but warning against accepting the omnipresence of *fengshui* in the conception and building of Chinese walled cities in general.

Acknowledging that it is possible to perceive a *fengshui* interpretation of a walled city's site and form does not necessarily mean that both emerged from the systematic application of *fengshui* principles. Indeed, it is likely that attention to general *fengshui* elements may have helped to restrain builders from making unwise ecological decisions. Furthermore, it is clear that *fengshui* tenets were applied to the plan and construction of individual—even groups of—structures such as houses or bridges within cities, even when there is no evidence of their comprehensive application to the city as a whole.

The External Form of Walled Cities

An examination of the pictographic and descriptive information contained in Chinese gazetteers concerning walled cities reveals an emphasis on certain aspects of external morphology, including shape, size, plan, outer walls, moats, and gates. While there are specific idiosyncrasies, there is an overriding resemblance among city walls. At the beginning of the twentieth century, a visitor to China could observe thousands of standing walls around cities, towns, and villages, but extant records tell us virtually nothing of the design and building of specific walls. Wall-building clearly was in the domain of artisans, who transmitted their techniques via apprenticeships, rather than vested in the literati, who might have produced written records. Archaeological evidence and creative scholarship today provide only suggested answers even to simple questions.

Since at least the Zhou dynasty (c.1050–221 BC), the idealized Chinese city was seen as having a square shape. Joseph Needham (1971, 73) suggests that there was

a strong cosmological element in the tradition, . . . connected no doubt with the ancient and widespread idea that the heavens were round while the earth was square. . . . The unsophisticated early

11

Chou [Zhou] cosmology surely visualized the heavens as round because the starry sky seems to the observer like a hollow spherical dome rotating continuously above him in a circular manner. The parallel idea that the earth was square surely arose from the simplest way of dividing the azimuth, into the four cardinal directions.

The idealized square shape of the Zhou-dynasty capital was laid out to measure 9 *li* on each side, oriented to the cardinal directions, with three gates on each of the four sides (Fig. 2.4). While literary records almost always underscore the orthodoxy of the square, in actuality shapes vary

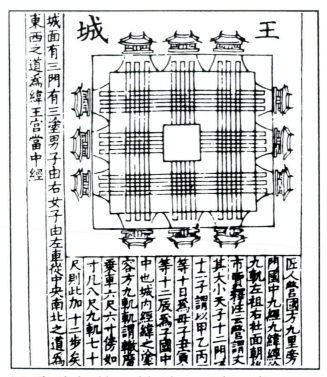

2.4 The idealized form of the Zhou capital according to *Kaogong ji*, as represented in a seventeenth-century drawing.

12

significantly from place to place, even when it would have been possible to construct a square. Of the one-hundred cities drawn in the late 1930s by Major Ishiwari Heizō of the Japanese Expeditionary Forces in China, shape varies from region to region. In general, there are more square and rectangular walls north of the Huanghe (Yellow River) than south of it, where shapes are more relaxed, breaking out from rigid angles to form more circular forms.

In the relatively flat and expansive lowland areas of northern China, it was relatively easy to create square or rectangular walled shapes that mimicked the similar shapes of individual courtyard houses found throughout the region. Chang'an, Xi'an, Beijing, and Pingyao, each discussed in the following chapters, all show evidence of this extraordinary geometrical regularity. However, as topography becomes much more irregular to the south of the Huanghe, city shapes too increasingly deviate from rectilinearity. A major factor influencing rounded edges and foreshortened sides in many areas of central China was the presence of sinuous trunk and tributary streams along whose banks walled cities were built. Even more irregular shapes emerged in the rugged areas of southern China, where confined sites appear to cradle walled settlements. Indeed, in a sample of nearly two-hundred walled cities in China, only 11 per cent were square, 9 per cent rectangular, and some 80 per cent with a variety of shapes, some of which were quite amorphous (Chiang 1980, 136).

Oval or circular walled cities were especially common in the low-lying riverine and coastal areas of Jiangsu and Zhejiang provinces, where square or rectangular walls could have been built relatively easily. An oval-shaped wall and moat were built around the market town of Shanghai in the mid-sixteenth century. The completed wrapping wall exceeded 5 kilometres in circumference, was nearly 4 metres high, and had six land and three water gates. Over the years, Shanghai's walls were improved but the walled city itself was not enlarged, and an extramural commercial city gradually developed to become a great metropolis, the 'Paris of the East'. The old settlement retained its walls until the Revolution of 1911, when the walls were summarily demolished in an effort to proclaim the city's modernization. A ring road replaced the line of the walls, existing even to today as visible evidence of the city's early oval form. It remains a puzzle as to why some southern walled cities, such as Hangzhou and Shaoxing, both in Zhejiang province, were portrayed in gazetteers as having orderly oblong shapes when they actually were highly irregular in form.

The relative size of walled cities generally followed their order in the administrative hierarchy, diminishing in size from imperial capitals to provincial capitals to county seats. Except for the county seats in Jiangsu province, which are especially large, the average size of the area contained within the walls of a county seat decreases from north to south in a striking correlation of size and relative location.

The remarkable variety of walled village shapes—square, round, oval, egg-shaped, semicircular, pentagonal, octagonal, and horseshoe—in south-western Fujian province demonstrates the creative range available in the construction of fortresses around even relatively small settlements (Plate 1). Although none of these fortresses is a 'walled city' in the sense that this form is discussed in this book, these remarkable walled structures—one of which is 90.6 metres in diameter—clearly express similar design elements in terms of construction techniques and plan. Some scholars have suggested that the earliest of these Fujian fortresses, like those still commonly seen in southern Jiangxi province, were once rigidly square (Plate 2). Round ones with constant radii, some specialists believe, were an evolutionary form that emerged as builders experimented with circular forms in order to maximize the amount of space enclosed within. A circular wall, it has been determined, is able to wrap approximately 27 per cent more interior space than a square wall of the same length, thus saving scarce building materials and facilitating modular construction of interior living space. (For a comprehensive examination of these walled village complexes in Fujian, Jiangxi, and Guangdong provinces, see Knapp 2000.)

Wall-Building

Although each walled city was not the solitary defensive feature of the area in which it was located, each city was indeed a well-fortified unit. Its high walls, whatever they were composed of, and moats, usually broad and deep, clearly provided an almost impregnable ring or set of rings around the settlement, protecting its inhabitants. Archaeological, historical, and contemporary evidence confirms that the most common method of wall-building has always been the tamping of earth, although the use of adobe and fired bricks has also had wide currency, especially since the fourteenth century. The imposing brick-faced city walls that survive today are mostly relics either of the Ming dynasty, a time of major repair, rebuilding, and new construction of city walls, or the subsequent Qing dynasty, rather than being survivals of more ancient forms.

The ease of raising tamped-earth walls made them an early and suitable means of protecting single isolated dwellings from the intrusion of humans and animals. Over time, short walls were connected and extended, perhaps even supplemented with other defensive features, in order to wrap villages and even towns. Impressive early examples of tamped-earth walls are common discoveries in excavated archaeological sites. Well before China was unified in the third century BC, high tamped-earth walls were used to mark the borders between kingdoms on the tawny plateaus, rugged mountains, and even fertile lowlands of north-western and northern China. Although Shihuangdi, the first emperor of the Qin dynasty (221–207 BC), is credited with initiating the construction of immense walls along the empire's borders, these were but crude precursors of the legendary Great Wall, whose form only emerged during Ming rule. The Great Wall is called in Chinese the 'ten thousand *li*-long wall' (*wanli changcheng*), but these ramparts are more multiple 'walls', in echelon, than a single line.

Although one can no longer witness the enormous scale of earlier great wall construction, traditional wall-building and foundation-forming using tamping techniques can still be seen in China's countryside. The method is described in Chinese as the *hangtu* (ramming earth) technique and is illustrated in early drawings (Fig. 2.5). Using a wide variety of soil types, the *hangtu* method, referred to in Western literature as *pisé de terre* and *terre pisé*, involves piling small amounts of freshly dug earth or other mixtures of soil and other materials into a slightly battered caisson before pounding the medium firmly. The *Shijing* (Book of songs) (Waley 1937, 248–9), from the early Zhou dynasty, provides a vivid portrayal of *hangtu* wall-building:

Dead straight was the plumb line.
The planks were lashed to hold the earth;
. . . .
They tilted in the earth with a rattling,
They pounded it with a dull thud,
They beat the walls with a loud clang,
They pared and chiseled them with a faint *p'ing, p'ing*;
The hundred cubits all rose.

16

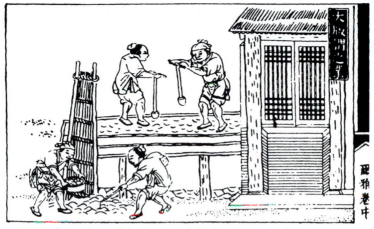

2.5 A traditional woodblock print of the *hangtu* method of wall construction, showing the shutter molds, collection of earth into baskets, and pounding using tampers.

Basic *hangtu* frameworks vary from place to place, but they make use of a restraining shutter mold consisting of a pair of H-shaped supports confined on their long sides by movable wooden poles or boards lashed together with thin rope or held by dowels. The thin poles and boards are easily and quickly raised up the sloping supports, level by level, as the ramming takes place. Each of the framing poles or boards must be periodically removed and cleaned of clinging earth in order to assure the stability of the rising wall.

Between the cavity of the timber or board shutters, freshly dug earth or a composite material—perhaps 10 centimetres thick at a time—is mixed with a small amount of broken grain stalks, paper, lime, and sometimes water or oil. In order to increase the bearing strength of this earthen composition filling, the earth is pounded with a stone or wooden rammer until it is uniformly compacted. A typical rammer is made of a heavy stone or wooden head, perhaps 25 centimetres wide, that is rounded on the bottom and attached to a projecting

17

wooden rod. Though heavier, they are somewhat similar to the pestles used to husk rice. Sometimes a transverse handle is threaded through the top of the wooden rod to ease the lifting and dropping of the rammer. Smaller tools of various sizes are used as well to insure that the soil mixture can be firmly packed. Before the movable shutters of the frame are raised, levelled, and clamped into place—to begin the process anew—a thin layer of bamboo strips or stone rubble is sometimes laid to encourage drying of the earthen core. This sequence is repeated, layer by layer, continuing until the desired height of a wall is reached. The wall is usually left with the rough impression of the timber or board frame.

Carl Whiting Bishop of the Freer Gallery of Art in Washington carried out fieldwork in China in the 1930s on the remains of the great earthworks of the ancient capital Chang'an, in an attempt to comprehend the magnitude of Chinese engineering achievements. Given that the city's perimeter walls ran some 25 kilometres in length, Bishop conjectured that the earth needed for their construction must have been borrowed from immediately adjacent areas, giving rise to broad and substantial moats—nearly 50 metres wide—as the earth was excavated. When Bishop carried out his survey, the remaining moats were only 3 metres deep, as a result of considerable siltation and collapse over the centuries. Because a section of one wall had been removed, Bishop was able to observe and measure its cross-section, revealing clearly the techniques employed in its early construction, as well as the changes that had occurred over time. He noted an inner tamped, layered, and very stable earthen core that was improved later by the addition of a fired-brick facing as protective revetments.

It is obvious from Bishop's findings that some of the sloughing off of the tamped earth core that occurred due to erosion by water and wind was periodically repaired by infilling with tamped earth and rubble. The greater damage and repair on the outer slope came as a result of the increased velocities of wind and water as they coursed against the wall's surface, especially in comparison with the better-protected inner face. The later facings of fired brick are similarly more regular on the inner wall than on the outer wall. According to Bishop, no stone plinth lay beneath the original weighty wall, but he presents no information concerning the possibility of an excavated below-grade foundation of rammed earth or other materials needed to carry the weight of the wall. He notes, however, the presence of a narrow and firmly packed berm along the outer wall. Its purpose, he writes, may have been to 'withstand the thrust of the vast mass of rammed earth above and behind it' whose height averaged 7.6 metres. Although Bishop only uses words to document his observations at Chang'an, he includes a similar profile of one of the walls of Beijing that reveals clearly the compacted layers of the rammed-earth core (Fig. 2.6).

2.6 A cross-section of the Beijing's city wall in the 1930s. The early tamped-earth core, subsequent repairs, and later brick facing are all apparent. Bishop 1938.

In spite of centuries of erosion by wind and water, the irregular lines and shapes of tamped-earth city walls, podiums of ancient buildings, and tomb tumuli are still apparent throughout the intensively cultivated plains of north-western China. Traces remain even though peasants over the years regularly borrowed soil from built-up sections of old walls to construct terraces and level fields for farming, in the process consuming the ramparts and remaking their agrarian landscapes. It appears that peasants recognized that organic material, such as dead grasses and roots, that were 'stored' within the layers of old earthen walls provided a source of enriched soil. In 'mining' old decaying walls, they were thus able to marginally enhance the fertility of their fields, steadily depleted by constant planting.

As early as the Zhou dynasty, tamped-earth or rubble walls were sometimes contained by headers and stretchers of thin adobe bricks, and this practice continued for many centuries. Some fired bricks began to be used as wall facing in the early years of the Han dynasty (206 BC–AD 220), but it was not until the opening of the tenth century, during the Tang dynasty (AD 618–907), that fired bricks were used in southern China to completely face city walls. During the Ming era in the fourteenth century, large fired bricks became relatively inexpensive and were widely used as facing on tamped-earth walls. Imposing brick walls became increasingly common in northern, central, and southern China over the next 400 years (Fig. 2.7). In Sichuan province, along the upper Yangtze, dressed sandstone, rather than brick, was widely used due to its easy availability.

Westerners who encountered the imposing forms of Chinese walled cities from the eighteenth into the twentieth centuries regularly commented on their indestructibility. In some cases, only the wall facing outward was reinforced with brick or stone, while the inner wall was merely

2.7 The crenellated ramparts of imperial Beijing, built with fired brick during the Ming dynasty, present an insurmountable face to the world outside. Martin 1900.

buttressed with an angle of tamped earth. This pattern is seen in the profile of the 6 metre tall wall surrounding Kaifeng, whose security was further reinforced with a 1.5 metre high parapet and a 15 metre wide moat (Fig. 2.8). Stone and brick parapets—called *nuqiang* ('female walls')—were frequently added as protective screens along the upper rim of many brick wall structures. Parapets were either plain on top or embattled, with open spaces punctuating the low

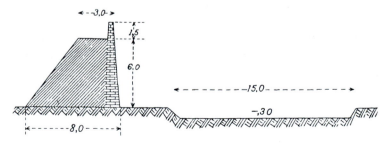

2.8 This cross-section of the wall wrapping Kaifeng, Henan province, shows a brick-faced outer façade but only a buttressed bank of earth on the inside. Ishiwari 1940.

protecting elevated fringe. With the introduction of cannon and rifles, some were pierced by embrasures, so that there was a slanting of the opening to increase the angle of sight. A common characteristic of Chinese walls is that they were slightly battered, that is, they were built sloping inward so that they were wider at the base than at their summit. In contrast, city walls in Europe and the Middle East often were built perpendicular to the ground.

As is seen in Figure 2.9, on top of the wall surrounding Dali, Yunnan province, at the beginning of the twentieth century was only bare earth adjacent to the brick parapet. The tops of the walls of major cities, however, were usually capped with dressed stone, such as the blocks of granite used to pave the top of the Ming wall around Beijing or fired bricks on the walls of other cities, in order to protect them from the elements. The tops of the walls of major cities were usually patrolled on a regular basis by soldiers and were not open as a public promenade.

Given the weight of the tamped-earth, brick, and stone walls described above, it is not surprising that it was

2.9 Although many walls had brick or stone pavements along the top, more were like Dali, Yunnan province, with short grasses growing on the surface. Geil 1911.

necessary to support each one's mass by laying a foundation. In those areas where the ground was moderately firm, the perimeter of the wall could be marked out and the earth beneath compacted using tampers made of wood and stone (Fig. 2.10). Compacted rubble, without any binding material, was used as the foundation for the walls of small and medium-sized cities throughout the country, and dressed stone was often used in the Jiangnan region, especially where tracts of land were regularly flooded or where the base was sandy. Unusually deep foundations, reaching 12 metres, have been excavated along some parts of the walls around Nanjing, while in other areas the walls sit directly on bedrock.

2.10 This late nineteenth century print shows the levelling of a building site. Workmen use tampers made of stone and wood to firm up the base, upon which slabs of foundation stone are placed. *Guding shujing tushuo* 1906.

The attentiveness of builders to the details of site conditions is revealed in comments concerning the preparations for wall-building around Taipei, Taiwan: 'work was not commenced on the city wall for several years, as the ground having been formerly a rice field was too soft to bear the weight of the heavy structure. Bamboos were, however, planted all along the prospective line of the wall with the idea that, when they grew up in some three or four years, the ground would be sufficiently strong and solid to bear the heavy wall of brick and stone' (Davidson 1903, 212). Even as this lengthy preparation was taking place, work began on the city gates, examination hall, the prefect's administrative offices (called the *yamen*), a Confucian temple, and a temple to the city god.

Lofty tamped-earth or brick-faced walls epitomize the great cities of imperial China. Even though most villages and small towns were ringed by only simple mud ramparts or bamboo palisades, however, some smaller settlements too were fortified with massive walls. Zhaojiabao, a village in Fujian province that was reputedly the refuge of the descendants of the last emperor of the Song dynasty (AD 960–1279), was ringed in the sixteenth century with a 6 metre high stone wall 2 metres thick. Each of its four massive gates suggests entry into a city rather than into an isolated village (Plate 3). Even as recently as the 1920s and 1930s, when rebellion, banditry, and general turmoil were common in northern China, high earthen walls were built around villages and towns in order to provide a level of enhanced security. Fortified residential complexes, some with towers and strong gates, continued to be built in the early part of the twentieth century in Jiangxi, Guangdong, and Fujian in southern China, where many are still standing today. Many contemporary rural settlements throughout China include *baozi* or *bao* (fortress) as part of their name, toponyms that remain even in the absence of the fortifications that once ringed the village or town.

As recently as the early part of the eighteenth century, bamboo palisades girdled small settlements in Taiwan, providing defence against unfriendly indigenes or contentious rival clans. These planted bamboo palisades were not precisely walls in the sense that they may be compared with the standardized and seemingly eternal walls of larger cities. Nonetheless, they did serve a similar function and often were of fairly large scale. Furthermore, the sites of palisaded non-agricultural settlements often evolved into increasingly important administrative centres, with the addition of more permanent earthen or brick-faced walls. About 1752, Taiwan Fu, today's city of Tainan, had a ringing wall that included growing bamboo clumps. The city's perimeter was also served by a fence-like stockade of tightly positioned logs, in addition to substantial gates with brick or stone bases capped with large wooden towers (Fig. 2.11).

Whatever their medium of construction, city walls decayed at a slow, barely perceptible pace, and in time they took on the look of dignified antiquity. Decay was usually hastened by the roots of vegetation that worked itself into the walls, in the process creating channels into which water could flow or ice could lodge to further speed up deterioration. Local officials were charged with the responsibility of maintaining walls and buildings, but it appears that in most areas in normal times only minimal maintenance and repair were performed, most often simply as a holding action against collapse. The walls around many cities indeed gradually took on the look of a patchwork, as different people at different times and with limited resources made repairs to them. In some cases, when a wealthy official exceeded his proper function by making an illegal appointment or committed bribery, his punishment might be making amends

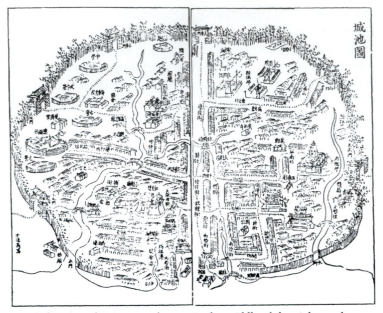

2.11 A drawing of Taiwan prefecture in the middle of the eighteenth century reveals the use of growing bamboo as well as a log stockade to wrap it. Seven brick or stone gates with their imposing towers are positioned along the simple wall. *Chongxiu Taiwan xianzhi*, *c.*1752.

by repairing the city wall at his own expense. It was out of the ordinary, and therefore noteworthy enough to be recorded in local gazetteers, when an official successfully repaired, restored, or enlarged a wall.

A circling moat was as much a convenient by-product of wall construction as it was a concrete defensive support. The complementarity between wall and moat may be seen in the readings of the terms: when *cheng* (city wall) and *chi* (moat) are read together, they indicate 'city'. Broad ditches usually were excavated as the borrow pits for the earth required to raise the walls. In northern China some moats were dry ditches, but in central and southern China moats were almost

26

always full of flowing water. Northern moats were also generally more narrow than were southern ones. Around Beijing and Taiyuan, for example, each moat was about 30 metres wide, while around Nanjing and Suzhou, on the other hand, the width was between 70 and 80 metres. Along the east side of Nanjing, the moat approached 200 metres in width. In general, depths were more uniform and generally did not exceed 5 metres. Moats in the north, with the notable exception of the one ringing Beijing, generally only served defensive functions and did not provide access into the city. In central and southern China, however, moats were usually fully integrated into the network of streams and canals criss-crossing the regions within which they were located. Between the moat and the city walls, a berm or apron of land of various widths was usually found. Western visitors to China in the nineteenth century frequently noted that this linear green space was often tidy and well-kept, affording a route for a pleasant walk away from the crowded spaces within the city.

Gate and Corner Towers

Gate and corner towers provided a prominent visual focus for all who entered a walled city and were also critical elements in the city's chain of defence. In some instances the gates were actually completed before the building of the walls, but more often they were completed simultaneously. Most cities had a minimum of four gates, with each opening towards one of the cardinal directions. The number of gates, however, varied significantly from city to city. Mancheng, in Hebei province, had only four, while Kaifeng during the Northern Song period (AD 960–1127) had thirteen. Generally, larger settlements, such as imperial capitals, had many more gates than did smaller cities and towns.

Each gate typically had a specific symbolic significance and an elegant poetic name that sometimes changed as the dynasties passed. Four gates normally reflected the symbolism of the cardinal directions, seasons, and winds. In this regard, the east gate represents the beginning of the annual and daily cycles, specifically spring and the diurnal rising of the sun at dawn. The south gate signifies summer, the period of maximum *yang* forces, as the winds from the south bring rainfall and warm temperatures. The west gate represents autumn and the waning of summer; it is through the west gate that the spirit of the ancestor travels to the Western Paradise. Finally, the north gate signifies winter, the period of maximum *yin*, and calamity. The north gate was normally kept closed in northern China, since this would block the penetration of cold winds.

If one can say that the number and significance of a city's gates along one wall are an indication of that city's orientation, then the fact that south walls often have more in number and larger gates than do other walls suggests that a city itself 'faces' south, as will be seen clearly in the discussion of Beijing in Chapter 4. This orientation conforms to that of temples, residences, pagodas, and palaces that similarly are oriented towards the life-giving south.

Three basic types of gates can be distinguished: simple gates, complex gates, and water gates. Simple and complex gates generally afford foot and cart traffic along a path or road and were found throughout the country. Water gates, on the other hand, were especially common in the Jiangnan region of central China, where canals and streams sometimes threaded themselves into and through a city's wall. Simple gates are essentially single gates, while complex gates involve the interlinking of two or more gates, each succeeding the other through openings in the wall. Simple gates were generally mere arched tunnels, 4 to 5 metres wide at their base and with their height ranging from 4 to 10 metres depending on the height of the wall itself (Fig. 2.12 and Plate 4). The archway could be recessed into the wall, aligned with it, or protruding, in order to provide a substantial platform upon which to raise a structure, such as the top-heavy gate tower. Since each gateway was a vulnerable point along the face of the wall, the panels that could be closed were usually quite strong. Rudolf Hommel (1937, 297–8), the great chronicler of the prosaic workaday technology of early twentieth century China, noted:

The wings of the gate are formed of roughly squared beams placed vertically aside one another and held together by several horizontal planks which pass through mortises in these upright beams. Through the center of the places of intersection of the vertical beams with the horizontal planks, a treenail is driven and thus the whole wing presents a remarkably solid structure. The hinging is the usual Chinese one, two pivots, one projecting upwards, the other

2.12 This simple gate through the wall of Dingxian, Hebei province, is arch-shaped, strongly constructed of fired bricks, and recessed into the thicker wall. Gamble 1931.

downward at the upper and lower gate corner, the upper one passing through a pierced projection of the stone lintel, and the lower one revolving in a round hole in the stone sill. The whole outer surface of the gate wings is imbricated with iron plates, hammered out at the anvil. The plates are nailed down and placed as we arrange slate roofing, the nail-hole always covered by an overlapping plate.

The entryways to many large cities, especially imperial capitals, were reinforced with ancillary structures in order to create a complex series of gates. The protruding *enceinte* or barbican that was formed strengthened the wall by creating layers of defence. Usually built in a semicircular or rectangular shape, complex gate assemblages were attached either to the inside or outside face of the wall itself in order to force turns in movement (Fig. 2.13). Sometimes, as in the case of the gates of Nanjing, the gateways were lined up, without any twisting, but the multiple passageways were expected to provide enhanced security by the doubling and

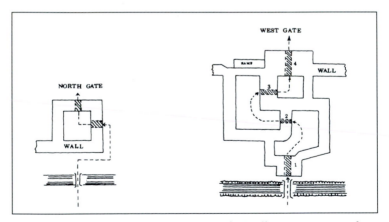

2.13 The purpose of these *enceinte* were to force all movement to make turns in order to reduce the speed and volume of any attack. Left: located on the inner wall of Taicang, Jiangsu province. Right: between the moat and the outer wall of Dingxian, Hebei province. Ishiwari 1940.

redoubling of the gates, as well as by the provision of raised areas for surveillance and for positioning archers (Fig. 2.14). These supplementary defensive gate structures are called *wengcheng* ('urn walls'), since they give the appearance in plan form—the view from above—of an earthen jar or urn. Although *wengcheng* were employed as early as the Han dynasty, they did not become popular until the Northern Song period, as innovations in weaponry called for improved defensive countermeasures. In some cases, as with two of the gates of Chengdu, in Sichuan province, and five of the gates of Guangzhou (Canton), the *enceinte* form is lunate and they are called *yuecheng* ('moon walls') to describe their simple geometrical form (Fig. 2.15).

Water gates, *shuimen*, were found principally in Jiangnan, near the mouth of the Yangtze. Throughout this densely populated, low-lying region, canals and streams typically were threaded into towns and cities for easy access into the

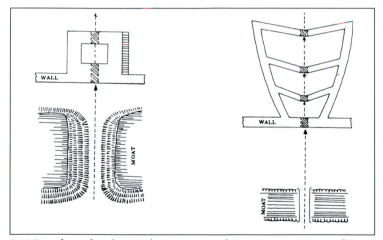

2.14 Portals are lined up in these two complex *enceinte* gates in order to provide added security by doubling and redoubling the gated entry points. Left: Guanghua Gate, Nanjing. Right: Shuixi Gate, Nanjing. Ishiwari 1940.

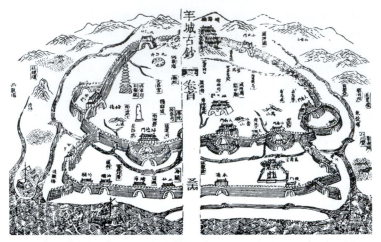

2.15 When the supplementary walls and gates are lunate in shape, as in the five principal gates of Guangzhou, they are called 'moon walls'. *Qiu Chishi Yangcheng guchao* 1806.

intramural areas by boats of all sizes. The special water gates that arched over the watercourses were usually secured at night by the lowering of a single-leaf iron gate or a picket-style fence which would not retard the flow of water. Many such water gates were about 5 metres wide, with at least 3 metres of clearance above the water line and a depth of about 2 metres. In Suzhou, Jiangnan's glorious canal city, there were twinned gates, adjacent openings allowing both water and land approaches into the city (Plate 5). Many cities throughout the country had small openings through their walls so that water could drain and sewage could pass into rivers and lakes outside.

When gates were closed at night, the unity of the city was complete. Unlike in the daytime, when each of the passageways and the areas immediately inside and outside were thronged with people, stalls, and carts, each gate stood silent over night under the watch of soldiers. Passage in and out was only permitted to a few privileged individuals who had been successful in securing a pass made of wood from an official.

Although the gates and city walls themselves were crafted of products of the earth, principally tamped earth, adobe or fired bricks, and rubble, the gate towers and corner towers that rose above them had a lighter, less massive character. Gate and corner towers were usually at least two, perhaps three, and sometimes four or more storeys high and conformed to the same architectural principles as did temples and houses. Structurally, each comprised a wooden framework that lifted the massive roof made heavy by clay roof tiles. Walls and screens were usually added to provide protection from weather. In addition to serving as vantage points for observation and fire command, gate towers also provided barracks and armories for guards and soldiers. Some gates were equipped with hidden or subterranean rooms in which weapons could be stored. Access to each gate tower was via an inclined ramp which abutted the gate, providing an approach for humans, carts, and horses. Corner towers, such as the one at Taigu, in Shanxi province, shown in Figure 2.16, were often reinforced, even though their appearance is of a relatively light pagoda. Occupied gate and corner towers provided locations for raising alarm and signalling commands if a crisis emerged. The piled tower above the wall of Ganzhou, in Jiangxi province, however, served principally as a prospect for viewing the eight notable sites associated with this riverside city (Plate 6).

Internal Form

Seen from a distance, Chinese walled cities presented a long unbroken profile that was punctuated only by gate and corner towers. Many appeared to be almost a natural growth from

2.16 This light and striking corner tower at Taigu, Shanxi province, provided an optimal location for surveillance and offered simple living quarters for guards. Fitzgerald 1935.

the soil beneath them, rising little in relation to their horizontal extent. Within the walls' massive embrace, each city and town had a character and activity of its own, even as all shared common features. Just as the form of the walls was connected to conscious decision, much of the appearance within was the product of design and precedent. According to classical sources, the orderly layout or interior plan of an imperial capital was to be as regular as the rigid walls that bound it. The right angles at the corner of a city and the sides themselves were to be fixed on the basis of a centre or midpoint that was established first for the settlement.

Whether gates or streets came first, of course, is academic, but the placement of one set of these predetermined the other. In great measure, the alignment of major streets was a function of the city gates that controlled access into the confines they marked, and convention usually fixed the alignment of major thoroughfares and principal buildings, as the relatively consistent ordering of these features throughout the empire demonstrates. Using calculations from the maps of one-hundred Chinese cities prepared by Ishiwari, four basic layout patterns can be differentiated.

Slightly more than 15 per cent of the cities mapped by Ishiwari have either a Greek (+) or a Latin (†) cross formed by intersecting streets running from north to south and east to west. The crossing thoroughfares usually run from opposing gates and are straight or nearly straight. Usually a drum tower to mark the passage of time was located at the intersection. This cross pattern, quite common on the North China Plain, approximates the ancient ideal Zhou form but, in fact, variations abound and are more common than precise cross-shaped forms (Fig. 2.17).

Close to 25 per cent of the cities mapped have a main thoroughfare running from east to west but no single road running from north to south from wall to wall. Instead, a road from the south gate only runs as far as the east/west thoroughfare to form a T-junction, while the road running from the north gate to the thoroughfare is offset to form an inverted T. This pattern is common in Hebei, Henan, Shanxi, and Shandong provinces.

Within Ishiwari's sample, 10 per cent of the cities display an I-shape pattern, with an arrow-straight thoroughfare running from the north gate to the south gate but no continuous street running from east to west. Broken street patterns are found in the plans of most cities and towns. Each of the gates feeds a route into the city, with those cities that have a large number of gates providing the greatest diversity. Many intersections are not at right angles and include many dead ends.

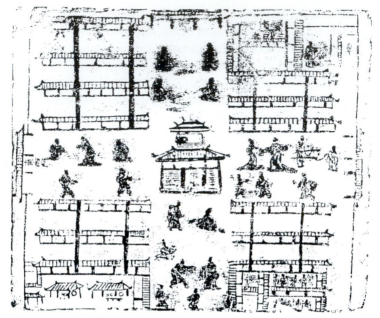

2.17 This rubbing from a molded brick from the Han period portrays an unknown city whose thoroughfares run from the east gate to the west and from the south gate to the north. Where they intersect space is provided for a drum tower, a focal point for marking time. Zhang 1985.

Even though a city might have a geometric centre, it was more common for there to be multiple areas of principal activity rather than a single central district of prominence. Temples, markets, and offices, located at specific nodes within the city, each provided a focal point for a zone of specific activities. In many larger towns, merchants and tradesmen clustered in certain neighborhoods so that there would be separate areas for selling tea, shoes, cooking oil, rice, cloth, books, medicines, funeral supplies, and the like, as well as for services such as those of potters, blacksmiths, barrel-makers, tailors, and pawnbrokers. Narrow signboards, about a half-metre wide and 4 metres long, were hung

36

perpendicularly from the eaves and advertised the goods or services provided by each narrow shop. In a single glance, one could see quickly the full scope of available business by easily reading the succession of shop signs on both sides of any commercial street. Street names often assumed the designation of the functional specialty of the street.

Space just inside or just outside the city gates provided locations for periodic markets for the sale of fresh produce and meats. Markets of this type in larger cities often were held daily, although their hours of operation were comparatively brief each morning, while those in smaller cities and towns operated on fixed schedules that were tied to a sequence that followed the lunar calendar. Goods and services were not provided only by shopkeepers and craftspeople working inside buildings and from temporary stalls. In addition, peripatetic hawkers purveyed a range of goods by peddling edible and durable goods throughout the course of each day, passing in front of virtually all residences. Mobile barbers and knife-sharpeners, and other entrepreneurs who catered to the service needs of households, offered doorstep service.

Except for the prominence of a drum or bell tower, it was rare to find structures in a Chinese city that were conspicuous because of their looming height. Such was the case with churches, cathedrals, and city halls in the West, which together created a punctuated skyline for the Western city. In contrast, if a Chinese city may be said to have had a 'cathedral' representing technological achievement, that 'building' was its walls, rather than any structure standing within the walls. Secular and religious buildings in China— both in cities and in the countryside—indeed share common architectural forms, and it is only the relative scale and proportion of their ground plan (not height) and ornamentation that produces a clear differentiation. When viewed from a distance in the open countryside beyond the walls, it was unusual to see any structures rise above the horizontal line except for the gate and corner towers that topped the battlements. In some instances, however, as with the Greater Wild Goose Pagoda associated with the Ci'en Temple in Tang-dynasty Chang'an, a seven-storey brick spire rivalled the towers atop the outer wall (Plate 7).

Since most walled towns and cities had an administrative function, there was order in the placement of each one's administrative structures. *Yamen* and even palace quarters were generally located near some major north/south route. Each building typically faced south, often in a receding complex of structures fronted by courtyards. Flanking side buildings served supplementary needs and formed quadrangular forms behind their own high walls. In this way, the administrative core was a walled city writ small and nested within the outer walls. Like intricately carved balls of ivory, in which many individual layers rotate freely, a nested hierarchy of elements—walls within walls—can be identified in each city. While this physical and functional layering is seen most clearly in an imperial capital, such as Beijing, it can also be observed in less-refined form in virtually any traditional walled city. Whether governmental or religious, each element sprawled rather symmetrically from its core structure, providing areas for the ceremonies, festivals, and fairs held throughout the calendar year.

A striking feature of many Chinese walled cities was the extent of the open areas beyond the buildings, including ponds, lakes, and canals, in addition to substantial areas of cultivated land (Fig. 2.18). With the length of a wall determined by a city's position in the administrative hierarchy, and core buildings completed near the centre of the city, built-up areas in a sense sprawled outwards from the centre towards the perimeter. Since most cities initially

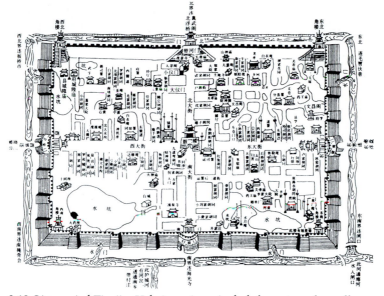

2.18 Qing-period Tianjin, Hebei province, included a rectangular wall, four gates oriented to the cardinal directions, and an intersecting set of thoroughfares. The moat that circumnavigated the city walls also fed substantial lakes within the city walls. He 1996.

enveloped more area than could be quickly covered by buildings, many urban landscapes initially had the appearance of a countryside bounded by a wall. The expansiveness of the unbuilt parcels is particularly striking in north and north-west China, where the fear of siege was mitigated by intramural farming that assured a regular food supply. In imperial and provincial capitals, expansive parks for the recreation of officials and local gentry usually occupied significant areas. The chain of artificial lakes that form a formidable band across Beijing's imperial landscape provided extraordinary garden-like spaces for the enjoyment of the imperial family.

Most Chinese cities, with perhaps the imperial capitals being the primary exception, embodied a patterned disorder in their internal form. Although the positioning of individual buildings was sanctioned by precedent, residential quarters generally spread in a *laissez-faire* fashion. Some Chinese cities were segregated into rich and poor areas that separated élites from the common people. In many cases, however, there was a mixing of social and cultural elements with an interdigitation of the structures housing them. In those cities with large non-Han populations or with significant numbers of in-migrants from other provinces, each group normally occupied a distinctive enclave.

Although major buildings were usually sited in relation to the symmetrical layout of the principal streets, this was not generally the case with residential lanes, which were laid out in relation to sometimes oddly positioned house lots. Besides employing *fengshui* to determine the siting of dwellings, the belief that, whenever possible, the main structures of a dwelling should face south meant that most lanes ran from east to west and had gates, each leading into a courtyard and house complex, only on the south wall. Secondary streets in Chinese cities rarely served as small-scale thoroughfares, as is often the case in the West. Rather, since their function was principally to provide access to a small number of residences, many were narrow and short, together resembling a labyrinth. Each served, as it were, as a capillary, permitting only trickles of pedestrians into and from the arterial thoroughfares. Many residential 'capillaries' actually were never dignified with a name of their own and traditionally—even today in some old cities—are identified only as alley, sub-lane, or lane of a major street for which they are but a tributary.

Over a long period of time, urban activities and settlement sometimes filtered beyond the walls, first adjacent to the main gates and then farther beyond along the roads leading to the city. If it was felt that these exclaves needed protection, subsidiary walls were built at some distance from the original walls.

This pattern of ethnic self-segregation was especially common during the Qing dynasty, when the conquering Manchus delineated Manchu from Han Chinese quarters. Some thirty-four such dual cities existed at the end of the eighteenth century. This pattern is seen clearest in the imperial capital of Beijing, discussed in Chapter 4, where the Manchus appropriated the totality of the nearly square Ming city they inherited and created an elongated outer city for Chinese. In the frontier regions of Inner Asia, attached walled suburbs were especially common, as the initial military 'forts' took on new functions and attracted multi-cultural populations. By the late nineteenth century, nearly two-thirds of China's frontier cities had multiple walls, while in the core areas of the country this development did not exceed 15 percent (Gaubatz 1996, 325).

3

Chang'an and Xi'an: Recalled Splendour

TOURIST GUIDES usually proclaim Xi'an as an ancient city that served as the imperial capital of eleven Chinese dynasties. The glory days of Xi'an, however, actually came much earlier than the walls that are still standing around the city suggest, at times when much larger walled cities, known by other names, were situated in its environs. These truly ancient and glorious walled cities include Xianyang, from which the Qin emperor first governed a unified China, Chang'an, capital of the Western Han (206 BC–AD 25) and some one-and-a-half times the size of contemporaneous Rome lying at the other end of the Silk Road, and the magnificent capital, also called Chang'an, of the Tang dynasty. Magnificent mausolea and temples, as well as unexcavated ruins, all impress upon the visitor the brilliance of these three dynastic periods, but virtually nothing remains of the walls that surrounded their imperial capitals and that lay some distance from the walls of today's Xi'an.

With the disintegration of the Tang dynasty in AD 907, Chang'an's walls, palaces, and residences indeed were all levelled, its nearly one million residents were driven away, and whatever wooden building materials could be salvaged were carried downstream by barge to new cities being built elsewhere by contending rulers. Chang'an was thereafter abandoned by all successive Chinese dynasties, which built new imperial seats of power at locations farther east and south of the former capital. Nearly five centuries after its abandonment, however, during the early years of Ming rule, the old location of Chang'an was deemed worthy of a prefectural capital, and a rectangular wall was built around a city that was renamed Xi'an: 'Western Peace' (Figs. 3.1 and

3.2). The name Chang'an (Eternal Peace), should be reserved for the grand Han and Tang capitals that were destroyed long ago and whose existence remains only in documents and memory. The fame of present-day Xi'an rests on the fragmentary remains of these long-vanquished walled cities of ancient times.

None other of China's imperial cities exceeds the magnificence of Chang'an during the Tang era, and the Tang capital compares well with Beijing during the 600-year span of the Yuan (AD 1271–1368), Ming, and Qing dynasties. Each of these two settlements had a long urban history, and indeed the grand walled cities of the late imperial period all were built near or on the sites of earlier capitals. While Chang'an and Beijing were certainly not unchanging as the centuries passed, each shared an unrivalled splendour for nearly a thousand years, a prominence anchored in the immensity of

3.1 Viewed from the air in the 1930s, this impressive Ming complex gate structure presents an impregnable barrier. Castell 1938.

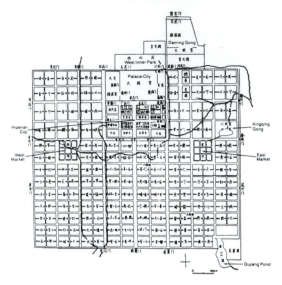

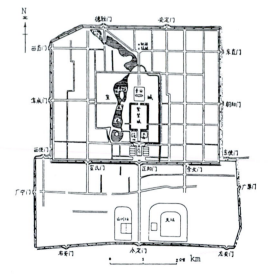

3.2 These two plans of Tang Chang'an (top) and Ming and Qing Beijing (bottom) reveal overall similarities but also differences in terms of their details. Steinhardt 1990.

their scale and layout, the magnitude of their urban population, and the grandeur of their external walls.

There is a superficial resemblance between Chang'an and the better-known Beijing as imperial capitals during the dynastic periods in which Chinese civilization flourished. As scholars have only begun to see clearly in recent years, however, there are as well profound differences in their origins and forms. In fact, as recently as the early 1980s, Chinese and Western writers stressed only the basic similarities of Chinese capitals throughout time, analysing their relationships to the prescriptions of the Zhou-period *Kaogong ji*, the outline of which was described above. It was not until the writings of the doyenne of Chinese architectural studies in America, Nancy Shatzman Steinhardt (1986, 1990), began to appear that an alternative view emerged.

As great capital cities, Chang'an and Beijing shared relatively common yet quite grand elements: layouts that were remarkably symmetrical and near perfect in the regularity of their geometry, an axial orientation tied to the cardinal directions, a fastidious pattern of internal wards, residential blocks, and gridiron-like streets, as well as prominent imperial palaces wrapped by magnificent outer and inner walls. Tang-dynasty Chang'an in the seventh century occupied some 84 square kilometres, eleven times larger than the present-day walled city of Xi'an that occupies only a portion of the same site and one-quarter larger than the greatest extent of walled Beijing during the Ming and Qing periods (Wu 1986, 30). New York City's Manhattan Island, by comparison, is only some 73.5 square kilometres in area, although it is longer from north to south and narrower from east to west than either Chang'an or Beijing.

Chang'an

The expansive and cosmopolitan Tang emerged out of the short-lived but powerful Sui dynasty (AD 581–618), inaugurating a 300-year period of political unity that was embodied in a vast empire whose international relations stretched across Central Asia and into Europe. In selecting a location for his imperial seat, the Sui founder probed the site of the great Western Han capital in the Wei River valley. For his new capital, however, which was called Daxing, he chose instead a location that had a better supply of water some 10 kilometres farther to the south. While design precedent— attention to early imperial forms—was important to founding emperors, geographical and geomantic considerations also framed the design of imperial Chang'an.

In laying out the capital, a roughly square ground plan for the city-to-be was superimposed upon a landscape that sloped from north to south, with the imperial palaces and principal buildings to be built on higher ground in the rear of the city complex. Taiji Gong, the palace city that was to serve as the emperor's residence, was built first and was followed next by Huang Cheng, a precinct known as the imperial city that functioned as the administrative centre for the empire. Both the palace city and the imperial city were wrapped with high walls, fragmented into building units, and connected as well as separated by strong gates. An ancestral altar was located to the east of the city centre, and one to the land and grain was placed on the west.

Radiating from this northerly nucleus of imperial residence and authority, the geometry of Daxing and its Chang'an successor emerged with a remarkable symmetry. Oriented to the cardinal directions, with north to its back and south to its front, the city took a compartmentalized and regular form. The enormous tamped-earth walls that were to form the perimeter of the city were built to intersect at right angles and to form a nearly square shape, with the distance east to west being 9.721 kilometres while the walls from north to south measured only 8.651 kilometres. A 155 metre wide principal axis road ran due south from the palace city through the imperial city and continued to Mingdemen (Bright Virtue Gate), located at a central position along the southern wall. This prominent avenue was reserved for use by the emperor and his processions alone. Mingdemen was one of three gates that lead into the city from the south. Three gates also breached the eastern and western walls, following *Kaogong ji* conventions, but five gates were cut into the back northern wall.

Within the nearly square frame of the outer walls of Tang-era Chang'an, a chessboard-like system of streets was strictly laid out. Three wide north/south and east/west avenues related to the gates along the east, south, and west walls were supplemented by narrower lanes that framed 108 blocks or wards called *fang*. *Fang* varied in size, but each was wrapped with tamped-earth walls that created a cell-like system of internal division within the city. Gates and sentries guarded access to each *fang*, in some of which certain craftsmen or foreign visitors concentrated, while the northern wards, which were larger than those in the southern part of the walled city, provided expansive spaces for the larger residences of the Tang nobility. A pair of markets, an East Market and a West Market, accentuated the symmetry and offered the bounty of local produce and products, as well as the luxury of foreign goods brought from the West along the Silk Road. Buddhist and Daoist monasteries, as well as Manichaean and Nestorian religious structures, were built throughout the city.

Two seventh- and eighth-century landmarks that can still be visited today—the Greater Wild Goose Pagoda and the

Lesser Wild Goose Pagoda—once stood prominently within the Sui and Tang walls, looming high above the city's residential neighborhoods (*see* Plate 7). The unprecedented scale of the walled area of Tang Chang'an meant that neither buildings nor markets were located outside the gates, as historically had often been the case in other Chinese cities; all was enveloped within the confines of the walls. Canals fed water into the city and served to drain it. It was only during the later Tang that Buddhist monasteries, opulent villas, and the fabled Huaqing hot springs were built outside the walled city in the hills to its south and east.

Chang'an epitomized the refinement of a golden age in which imperial political power surged and prosperity advanced in unprecedented fashion. Throughout the Tang, arts and architecture flourished, as did literature and scholarship of all types. In 634, the Tang emperor ignored the symmetry of the developing city by constructing a trapezoidal palace complex replete with main and many subsidiary halls. Called Daming Gong, this expansion of imperial architecture northward beyond the Sui walls created a complex of multistoreyed and multicolored wooden structures. The motivation for this expansion seems to have been dissatisfaction with flooding that had occurred within the imperial precincts inside the Sui walls. Built on higher ground, the irregular Daming palace complex satisfied practical concerns while deviating significantly from the regularity of the imperial city that spread before it.

It is remarkable that an imperial metropolis of this magnitude took its fundamental shape in less than forty years. While the essential geometrical form of the regal capital of the short-lived Sui dynasty endured throughout the succeeding Tang period, the Sui name Daxing was itself eclipsed by the name that the Tang emperors gave to the city they inherited. 'Chang'an' echoed the name given by the Han emperors to their nearby capital, establishing an historical connection to the great Chinese empire of earlier times.

The glorious configuration of Sui Daxing and Tang Chang'an made it a model, whose regular form and overall structure were adapted at locations some distance from the source. 'Ironically,' Steinhardt tells us, 'survivals in replica beyond China's borders have accounted for some of our knowledge of what has not endured on Chinese soil.' Most notable among these adaptations were the rebuilding in Korea of the Silla capital of Kyongju in AD 601 and the building in Japan of Heijō-kyō, now the city of Nara, in 710 and Heian-kyō, present-day Kyōto, in 794, all of which echoed elements of Sui Daxing and Tang Chang'an. The details of these cultural transfers of abstract ideas and concrete realities to Japan and Korea, as well as to locations beyond the Great Wall, including the possibility of pre-Sui and Tang influences, is beyond the scope of this book but are well described by Steinhardt (1990, 108–18).

Xi'an

No Chinese dynasty after the fall of the Tang imperial house returned to the location of Han Chang'an, Sui Daxing, or Tang Chang'an for its imperial capital. Today, the important city of Xi'an, whose origin only reaches to the Ming dynasty, is situated across but a small portion of the historical space once occupied by the great walled metropolises of earlier times. Indeed, the Greater Wild Goose Pagoda—once within Chang'an's walls—today stands outside Xi'an's south gate as a melancholy marker of past eminence, towering above simple country houses and fields rather than the neighborhoods of a great imperial capital.

Xi'an, nonetheless, is still usually referred to as an 'ancient walled city', one whose contemporary existence is used to validate the extraordinary continuity of Chinese civilization (Fig. 3.3). Its environs indeed include not only the vestiges of Qin, Han, Sui, and Tang imperial glories but also offer clear evidence of continuous occupancy since neolithic times. Here in southern Shaanxi province one can visit the remains of the neolithic village of Banpo, countless Han-dynasty tumuli, and the unexcavated tomb and extraordinary excavations of terracotta warriors and horses associated with the great unifier, the first emperor Qin Shihuangdi. One can also see Tang-dynasty sculpture and imperial tombs, Ming-dynasty walls, gates, and a bell tower, Islamic quarters and mosques, as well as sites of China's twentieth-century revolutionary history. The city itself, however, has never regained the celebrated eminence of its form as glorious Chang'an during the Tang period. Over the years, the great Tang walls and splendid palaces were demolished, or fell into disrepair and disappeared.

3.3 A rounded outlier finishes a 'corner' of the Ming wall surrounding Xi'an. Original photograph used with the permission of Nancy Shatzman Steinhardt.

During the Ming dynasty, new rectangular walls of a much-diminished city were built. Recent repair work on the walls affirm that some sections of the Tang wall indeed were buried within the core of the 'new' Ming wall (Plate 8). It is these majestic brick-faced walls of the Ming dynasty that endure today and suggest only in a quiet way the grandeur of Xi'an's past glory (Fig. 3.4). Ming and Qing Xi'an presented a symmetrical rectangular plan with two intersecting streets laid out according to the cardinal directions. Where they intersect, a massive bell tower, built in 1582, still stands in the centre of a traffic circle. During the Qing dynasty, Manchu troops and their families were garrisoned in the north-east portion of Xi'an, secluded behind a new walled quadrant (Fig. 3.5). As imposing as are Xi'an's surviving walls, it is striking to note that they only wrap an area approximately one-sixth the size of Sui Daxing and Tang Chang'an!

3.4 This simple side gate along Xi'an's east wall displays the magnitude of its tamped-earth, brick, and stone construction.

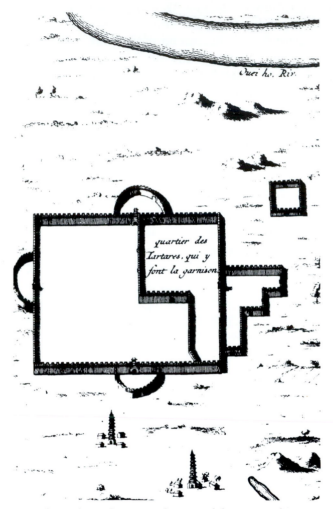

Ouei ho. Riv.

quartier des Tartares, qui y font la garnison.

3.5 This eighteenth-century drawing of the rectangular walled city of Xi'an shows clearly the delineation of a Manchu quarter in the eastern part of the city, as well as the reinforced *wengcheng* that protect each of the four gates. Outside the southern walls are the two pagodas that once were inside Tang Chang'an. Du Halde 1736.

4

Beijing: Magnificent Imperial Capital

CONTEMPORARY BEIJING, like Xi'an, has a long and complicated history, with many names applied to it and many distinct settlements occupying different sites at different times. Historians point to the fossil remains of Peking Man, recovered from the dawn of human evolution in Zhoukoudian to the city's south-west, as evidence of very early occupancy—well before there was any city. The important historical sites for imperial Beijing, however, took form on the northern edge of the North China Plain, a substantial distance from the cradle areas of Chinese civilization.

Urban settlement in the immediate environs of today's Beijing has many overlapping layers that can be traced first to the Zhou dynasty, some three thousand years ago, and which began with the building of a wall around a city known as Ji. Over the centuries, other periods of imperial capital-building brought walled cities to the area, but virtually all of these fell into oblivion. Prominent cities built on or near the site include auxiliary capitals built by non-Han rulers from the border areas, who established Chinese-style dynasties during periods of disunity. Among the best known of these Chinese-style capitals was the tenth-century Nanjing (also called Yanjing) of the Liao dynasty (AD 916–1125) and the twelfth-century Zhongdu of the Jin (AD 1115–1234). Both of these cities were wrapped with multiple concentric walls and included compounds with large halls, palaces, and residences. Jin Zhongdu, especially, provided a precursor physical form that is still recognizable in the Beijing we see today, even though its palaces and walls all were burned and reduced to rubble.

It was only as a result of the Mongol conquest of China in the thirteenth century that a magnificent imperial city began fully to emerge. The Mongol conqueror Khubilai Khan built the capital of his pan-Asian empire in proximity to earlier Chinese settlements at a strategic location inside the Great Wall, an achievement of capital-building celebrated by Marco Polo in his descriptions of the fabled Cambaluc (Khanbaligh or 'Khan's City'). Although Khubilai saw himself as 'Khan of the Mongol Khans', he was also in fact emperor of China. Accordingly, while the Khan's capital was built by and for the non-Han 'barbarian' conquerors from the steppes, who had defeated the Chinese Song imperial system after prolonged warfare, his capital was not a Mongol-style settlement. Somewhat ironically, the new city 'adhered more closely to a classical Chinese city plan than any imperial city built within China's borders which had come before it' (Steinhardt 1983, 137).

Given the Chinese name Dadu (Great Capital) when made the imperial seat of the Yuan dynasty in 1272, in its conception, construction, and style the new settlement reflected a host of past city-building influences, even as it eventually became the embryonic form for the Beijing one sees today. Early models for Yuan Dadu drew inspiration not only from Mongol experiences in building urban settlements in the borderlands, and the influence of city construction by other non-Chinese tribes during the tumultuous times after the fall of the Northern Song, but it revealed as well the conscious pursuit of Chinese urban design by the Mongols in order to legitimize their imperial rule.

Yuan-dynasty Dadu was conceived on a foundation of near-perfect geometrical shapes, echoing canonical forms that had been spelled out in the *Kaogong ji* but which had up to that point never been fully realized in Chinese imperial plans. The exterior wrapping wall stretched some 28.6 kilometres along a rectangular perimeter that was longer from north to south than from east to west. Built along a north/south axis, the walls were oriented to the four directions and essentially were completed before the palaces and other internal buildings were constructed. Three symmetrically placed gates were built along the east, south, and west walls, while only two gates pierced the back wall in the north. As in Chang'an, broad roads ran from the eastern gates to the opposing gates on the west city wall. Subsidiary roads gave shape to neighbourhoods that were isolated throughout the grid-like plan. Unlike in Chang'an, where the palace precinct was situated deep within the city at a northern location, the walled heart of Yuan Dadu was located to the south of the city's centre marker, situated to facilitate the placement of the wrapping main walls.

Yuan Dadu did not fully conform to the dictates of the *Kaogong ji*, which called for a concentric series of walls with the emperor's palace at the centre, but it nonetheless had a nested configuration with the palace city set within the imperial city. While adopting Chinese architectural forms for their palaces and temples, the Mongol rulers also introduced some elements, such as large felt tents or yurts, that recalled for them life on the grasslands. As a result, within the walled interior precincts of Dadu, it was possible for the Mongol rulers of China to continue to rehearse private rituals more appropriate to the expansive natural steppes of Mongolia from which they originated than to the settled life of an imperial capital.

Mongol rule of China in the form of the Yuan dynasty lasted just short of a century. To help feed the growing population in the northern capital and its environs, the Mongol emperors extended the Grand Canal from the fertile rice-growing areas in the south to the northern capital. Artificial watercourses, ponds, and a substantial lake provided visual delight for Dadu's residents, as well as critical water resources needed for the large population. Just as the securing of sources of drinking water remained a problem in Beijing for centuries to come—even in the present day it is addressed by an extensive system of canals, ponds, and lakes—the shape and structure of the subsequent Ming and Qing imperial capitals retained the essential elements of those bequeathed by the barbarian Mongols.

The tamped-earth walls of Dadu were strikingly battered, with widths at the base of as many as 24 metres but measuring only 8 metres at the top. It is said that reed mats were attached to the walls in order to protect them from damage from summer downpours. Today, there is little visible evidence of Yuan Dadu aside from remnants of the earthen ramparts of the northernmost earthen wall, located between Beijing's third and fourth ring roads. Remnants of one of Dadu's eleven gates was unearthed in 1969 when the Xizhi gate was being dismantled in order to create new traffic patterns. Regrettably, these relics of the thirteenth-century Yuan gate were merely photographed and measured before they, too, were levelled (Fig. 4.1). In contrast, relics of the Mongol astronomical observatory are still at a location,

4.1 Discovered during construction in 1969 near the Xizhi gate in western Beijing, remains of a Yuan-era gate were unearthed but subsequently destroyed. Zhang 1985.

chosen by Khubilai's Persian astronomers around 1280. This ancient observatory, with many new instruments, was subsequently incorporated during the Ming period into a platform above the brick-faced wall.

Even as the Mongols became increasingly sinicized in thought and action, their dynastic hold on China gradually weakened, especially in the later decades of their rule. Increasing failures in imperial policy, rebellions in Tibet and Manchuria, corruption of the bureaucracy, inflation, floods along the Huanghe, and unsuccessful military expeditions against rebel bands throughout southern China all helped eventually to undercut their rule. In 1368, the insurgency of the fabled Zhu Yuanzhang drove the Mongols from their capital at Dadu and flattened much of it.

In establishing a new dynasty called Ming, with the former rebel Zhu now ruling as the Hongwu emperor, the empire's new leaders abandoned the site of the Mongol imperial capital. In its place, they established the base of their power at Nanjing (literally, Southern Capital) in the lower Yangtze valley and began to surround it with imposing walls, a subject discussed in the next chapter. Unlike the geometrically drawn walls of northern capitals, however, which were to be constructed on sites that were often quite flat, the walls of sprawling Nanjing were irregular and curved here and there as they traced lines along the rugged hills surrounding the new imperial seat.

The old Yuan capital, now renamed Beiping (Northern Peace), was granted to the Ming emperor's fourth son, who began immediately to change the form of the city even as its residents attempted to rebuild those portions ravaged during the change of regime. Recognizing the diminished stature of the city and the reduced forces to defend it, extensive portions of the wall that framed the northern tracts of Yuan Dadu were demolished. This foreshortening of the vast, relatively open areas by a distance of 2.5 kilometres, representing a reduction of about one-third of the original Mongol domain, was accomplished by destroying massive tamped-earth walls as well as four gates. Two of the demolished gates were located in the northern wall, and two were in the northern portions of the eastern and western walls. The two northern gates, necessarily, had to be rebuilt in the newly constituted northern wall. With these modifications, only the southern wall maintained three gates. None of the remaining gates was matched with an opposing one as part of a symmetrical pair.

The founding Ming emperor's fourth son became the third Ming emperor, Yongle, in 1403. Forsaking his northern seat and taking up residence at the imperial capital in Nanjing, he renamed Dadu 'Beijing' (Northern Capital), designating it a dual capital of the regime, to be used when he was on tour. In an attempt to reproduce the sound of 'Beijing,' Europeans and others called this new capital 'Peking' and 'Pékin' until recent times.

After consideration of many factors, the Yongle emperor decided in 1420 to formally move the imperial seat back north to the base of his earlier power. He declared, 'The site is strong and secure, the mountains and rivers protect it well, the ten-thousand nations lie on its four sides. It is a place favored by sound reason, by the mind of heaven and by exact divination' (Meyer 1991, 22). This reversion plan was nearly upset, however, by the Emperor's early death. His successor, the Hongxi emperor, also decreed the capital should return to Nanjing but he, too, died unexpectedly. Nonetheless, it was subsequently affirmed that the intentions of the eminent Yongle emperor were to continue the celebrated site of Beijing as the Ming dynastic capital.

While the majestic configuration spelled out for Beijing by the Yongle emperor at the beginning of the fifteenth

1. Imposing walled village complexes in south-western Fujian province include round and square shapes, the remains of some of which date to the thirteenth century.

2. With their corner towers, square walled fortresses in southern Jiangxi appear like miniature walled cities.

3.   Some smaller settlements, like Zhaojiabao in southern Fujian province, had imposing walls and gates similar to those of large cities.

4. The North Gate of Taipei, Taiwan, had a brick base through which an entryway led into the city, and the arched opening on the second level was linked to the top of the adjacent wall. In 1966, the surviving gate still dominated the traffic circle in which it was located.

5. The Pan Gate in the city of Suzhou includes a double water gate as well as a nearby land gate with a tower above it. Original photograph used with the permission of Joseph Cho Wang.

6.　Bajing Terrace was built atop the north-western corner of the city walls surrounding Ganzhou, Jiangxi province, between 1056 and 1063 as a prospect for viewing distant vistas.

7.　Sixty-four metres high, the Greater Wild Goose Pagoda was built in AD 652 within the southern walls of Chang'an, the Tang capital.

8. This view of the battered interior southern wall of Xi'an looks towards a tower set upon a wide podium.

9. Viewed from the north-west, the two towers of Zhengyangmen are not connected; they are instead sitting on the south end of Tiananmen Square and are divided by a major east/west thoroughfare.

10. Viewed from the southern tower across the thoroughfare, the completely restored northern tower of Qianmen has been brought back to its Qing-dynasty colours.

11. Viewed obliquely from the south-east, the transformation of Tiananmen from imperial gateway to socialist podium is clearly seen. Tiananmen rests today on the edge of Chang'an Boulevard and is fronted by sculpted gardens as well as Tiananmen Square.

12. The U-shaped structure known as the Meridian Gate today serves as the location for purchasing tickets into Beijing's Forbidden City. Throughout the early 1990s, work continued on the restoration of the plaza in front of the gate.

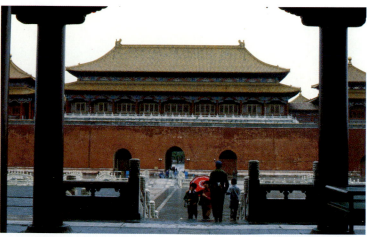

13. Looking south from the Gate of Supreme Harmony, the final gate before entering the walled imperial palace complex, one sees the looming backside of the Meridian Gate.

14. The Bell Tower in the northern portions of Beijing is at the end of the 8 kilometre long central axis and sits just north of the Drum Tower.

15. More slender than a traditional pagoda, the Monument to the People's Heroes is an obelisk of powerful symbolic and commemorative significance.

16. Although much of the walls around Nanjing have weathered and become overgrown, their substantial brick face remains.

17. Viewed from the west gate of Pingyao, each of the projecting terraces rhythmically juts out as a defensive feature.

18. The parapet along the outer wall of Pingyao contrasts with the battered slope of the inner wall.

19. By 1990, Taipei's North Gate had been wrapped with overpasses that nearly submerge its existence. Even at ground level, the increasing volume and size of the passing vehicles diminishes the gate's overall prominence.

century was to endure well into the twentieth, long after the days of imperial China had come to a close, still to occur was some significant reshaping of the outer walls that further transformed the city. The earlier foreshortening of the northern walls to exclude vast open spaces was followed between 1419 and 1421 by the movement of Dadu's original southern wall nearly a kilometre farther south in order to make room for a host of new *yamen* that were built just outside the southern gate of the imperial city. Today this cluttered administrative area of Ming and Qing China is no longer in evidence; instead, the space is occupied by the vast expanse known as Tiananmen Square. The movement of the southern wall also, and not incidentally, led to a repositioning of the imperial and palace cities, placing them at a relatively more central and concentric position. As new palaces, as well as the Drum and Bell towers, were being built in 1420, the palace city itself was shifted somewhat to the east of the axis of Yuan Dadu in order to affirm a new north/south axis.

The sumptuous palaces visitors see today in the complex known as the Forbidden City or Palace Museum are spread within a 73-hectare complex—some 960 metres from south to north and 760 metres from east to west—and are all relics of the Yongle emperor's grand redesign of Beijing. In addition to imperial structures, a magnificent complex gate structure, called Zhengyangmen, was constructed as the main— southern—entrance to the Ming capital. After the death of the Yongle emperor in 1424, succeeding emperors continued to improve the walls in terms of size and materials. In addition to facing all the walls and gates with bricks, complex counterscarps and embrasured towers were constructed in order to strengthen many of the gates.

Imperial Beijing of the early Ming period, with nearly 24 kilometres of ringing walls, assumed a shape closer to that of a square than at any time in its history, but this near-perfect form was about to change. In the mid-sixteenth century, a major effort was made to expand further the capital's area in order to protect the thriving commercial area that was developing outside its southern wall and to increase security against Mongol horsemen who continued to harass the new rulers. Initially, an additional outer wall was envisioned that would circle completely the square walled city. Various circumstances, based upon human and material resources, however, resulted in the project being aborted in 1553. Only the outer extra wall on the southern edge of the city was completed at the time, and it was then connected to the older wall by short perpendicular segments. This addition, together with the nearly square city to its north, bestowed upon Beijing the inverted T-shape seen in Figure 3.2.

In addition to enclosing newly established residential areas and commercial districts, including flower, vegetable, book, mule, jewel, furniture, tea, and meat markets, the elongated walled area brought within it the once remote but exquisite imperial precincts known as the Temple of Heaven and the Temple of Mountains and Rivers. In addition to three gates that led north to the walled city, seven others opened to areas beyond the new walls. The original area in the north that held within it the imperial precincts became known as the Inner City (Neicheng), while the new southern walled district was called the Outer City (Waicheng), a distinction that reveals the implicit hierarchy in the architectural design (Fig. 4.2). The efflorescence of Beijing during the Ming dynasty reflects the glory of a significant period in the development of Chinese civilization, but it, like other turns in the dynastic cycle, was not to last forever.

Throughout the sixteenth and seventeenth centuries, the vibrancy of Ming power withered, as social unrest and peasant rebellions increased across the land and the military

4.2   A corner tower along Beijing's crenellated wall at the end of the nineteenth century. Martin 1900.

power of non-Chinese 'barbarians' grew along its northern borders. From beyond the Great Wall, which the Ming emperors had reinforced as a means to restrain advances from beyond, Manchu strength surged. By 1629, Manchu forces were at the gates of the Ming capital, even as Chinese rebels also continued to strike out at the imperial forces. In late spring 1644, a Han rebel leader occupied Beijing and the last Ming emperor committed suicide by hanging himself in the palace gardens to the north of the palace city.

With the establishment in 1644 of the Manchu-dominated Qing dynasty, Beijing was again designated as the imperial capital, and thus the grand Ming walled city passed to the new rulers without any of the destruction that had in the past usually accompanied dynastic transitions. The new Manchu rulers, however, banished Han Chinese from the Inner City that surrounded the imperial precincts, forcing them into the rectangular Outer City to its south. Each of eight Manchu military groups, called banners, were stationed with their families in the area around the imperial city that had been evacuated by its Chinese residents. It was this action that led Western observers to label the Outer City the 'Chinese City', while the Inner City was called the 'Tartar (or Tatar) City', misapplying a descriptive term more suitable to describe Mongols or Turks than Manchus. During the unprecedented sixty-year reigns of the Qing emperors Kangxi (r.1662–1722) and Qianlong (r.1736–95), repairs of Ming structures continued apace, but no substantial changes occurred in the form of the city walls (Fig. 4.3). Many gates and other structures, however, were refurbished and renamed.

The scale and grandeur of Ming and Qing Beijing—across a span of more than five centuries—elevated its reputation to a position of extraordinary significance. Western visitors from the eighteenth through the twentieth centuries wrote glowingly of the city's exquisite imperial architectural ensembles, including palaces, temples, gardens, and,

4.3 The view along the crenellated parapets of Beijing's wall near Zhangyimen. Siren 1924.

certainly, the impressive walls that surrounded them all. J. B. Du Halde, for example, wrote in 1736 of 'the width, height, and beauty of the walls', calling Beijing's 'superb, worthy of the capital of the greatest empire in the world'. Du Halde's outline map of the city, shown in Figure 4.4, highlighted Beijing's walls, gates, and battlements, identifying some twenty-three important sites, principally those in the imperial precincts. The map emphasizes the

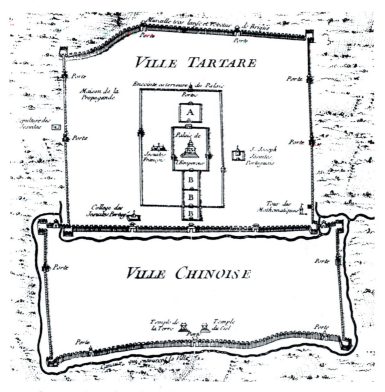

4.4 Showing the T-shaped city that emerged from Ming efforts to build another wall around Beijing, this map represents the ethnic segregation during the Qing period that separated the new Manchu rulers in the north from the Chinese city in the south. Du Halde 1736.

inverted T-shaped plan of the city without calling attention to the symbolic power of its spatial organization, particularly the axis that runs from south to north.

To comprehend the grandeur of imperial Beijing, one must read the progression of key structures and spaces along this north/south axis. In distance, the path from the southern-most gate to the Three Great Halls and the emperor's throne in the Forbidden City is relatively short, but the symbolic distance is substantial. A traverse of the full length of this impressive axial route reveals the coincidence of plan, structures, and symbolic meaning, a course that only the emperor himself could actually pass along. As the twenty-first century begins, many of the structures and some of the gates remain as emblems along this line, while others are recalled by name even as their material form has disappeared. Because there were some variations in names over the course of the Ming and Qing dynasties, this discussion will cite only those names commonly in use as the Qing dynasty waned at the end of the nineteenth century.

After 1553, the formal approach to the city was through Yongdingmen in the southern wall of the Outer City, a gate that lead northward across a broad avenue that separated the walled Temple of Heaven on the east from the Temple of Mountains and Rivers on the west. After crossing the Tianqiao (Heavenly Bridge), which came to mark an entertainment quarter during Qing times, the road narrowed as it approached the imposing Zhengyangmen (Gate That Faces the Sun Directly).

Zhengyangmen itself was a composite fortified gate, or barbican, with lofty superstructures above them that were connected by walls to form an interior courtyard (Fig. 4.5, Plates 9 and 10). Three gates passed through a lobate wall topped with a tower building. The central gate was opened only for the use of the emperor when he travelled from his

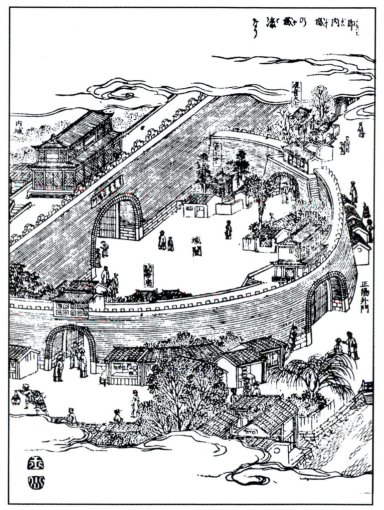

4.5 This Ming drawing of Zhengyangmen emphasizes its crescent-shaped *wengcheng* and battlements, as well as the two towers above its outer and inner gates. Arlington and Lewisohn 1935.

palace to the Temple of Heaven for ritual purposes, while the other two gates were used every day by common people. Chinese call complex gates of this sort *wengcheng*, since in plan view they appear like a globular earthenware jar. The Zhengyangmen complex protruded from the wall in a somewhat semicircular form that provided additional strengthening at this vulnerable location. In the event of an attack, all gates on both sides of the open courtyard would be closed. If the outer gate failed and troops were to penetrate the enclosed courtyard, they would find themselves vulnerable to attack by the archers assembled along the upper ramparts of the confining walls.

Zhengyangmen today, as at the later part of the Qing dynasty, is generally referred to as Qianmen, 'Front Gate'. During the imperial period, the gate did not lead to the expansive Tiananmen Square that one sees today but instead into a much more restricted area that contained a freestanding gate. This structure was earlier called 'Great Ming Gate', and then later during the Qing dynasty 'Great Qing Gate'. After 1912, during the Republican period, it was renamed 'Central Flowery Gate', from the Chinese name of the Republic of China. This gate opened on to a T-shaped 'thousand paces' walled imperial way and then to an elongated open space that eventually reached the magnificent Tiananmen (Gate of Heavenly Peace) and the entrance of the imperial city. This progression of gates is shown in Figure 4.6 as it was still standing at the end of the Second World War. By the time of the photograph, however, the wrapping walls that connected the two gate towers of the Zhengyangmen barbican had been removed to facilitate motorized traffic. The linkage between the double Zhengyangmen, the magnificent Tiananmen, and the visible imperial palaces beyond inscribes the symbolic longitudinal axis of the imperial processional path.

4.6 In the years before the founding of the People's Republic in 1949, the area between Zhengyangmen and Tiananmen was still marked by open space at its core and *yamen* on both sides. The low Da Qingmen lay just beyond the double Zhengyangmen, whose battlements had long since been removed to facilitate motorized transport. Original photograph by Dmitri Kessel, used with the permission of Time-Life Books.

Just before entering the Tiananmen gateway, with its five vaulted passageways piercing its thick walls, five sculptured-marble arched bridges cross a narrow waterway that complements a similar one inside the Forbidden City. Tiananmen and its lofty tower was first erected in 1420 as formal entry to the imperial city. It was rebuilt in 1651 in order to repair the damage incurred with the change of

67

dynasty. With its crimson walls and yellow glazed-tile double roof, the gate tower is a fine example of palace-style wooden architecture. Nine bays wide and five bays deep, the lofty and impressive structure served as an elevated platform from which imperial edicts were issued.

Tiananmen, as can be seen in Plate 11, soars some 33.7 metres above the open area beneath it. It was here from a symbolic imperial structure that Chairman Mao Zedong proclaimed the founding of the People's Republic of China in October 1949. Today the 10 metre high crimson walls serve as the backdrop for two Socialist proclamations, 'Long Live the People's Republic of China' and 'Long Live the Unity of the People of the World', that frame an immense portrait of the Chairman. Before the twentieth century, only the emperor could pass through the central gate that pierces Tiananmen. Today, anyone may walk leisurely through the 45-metre tunnel-like portal that leads first to another 45 metre long tunnel through the massive gate known as Duanmen (Uprightness Gate) before reaching the enormous stone-paved courtyard that lay before Wumen, the imposing entry to the imperial palace itself.

Only two hundred short paces separate Duanmen and Wumen (Meridian Gate), so named to accentuate its critical position astride the longitudinal line marked by the sun at noon, but the majesty of what is still hidden beyond becomes tantalizingly palpable. The Meridian Gate, with five enormous doors, is an immense inverted U-shaped structure with double eaves that soar above its formidable mass beneath. More than imposing architecture, as is seen in Plate 12 and in a fanciful nineteenth-century engraving in Figure 4.7, this gate, the 11 metre high walls that ran outwards from it, as well as their flanking moat, presented an impregnable barrier for the Forbidden City, the 'great within' at the centre of the Chinese world (Plate 13).

4.7 Originally built in 1420 and restored in 1647 and 1801, the Meridian Gate was used by the emperors to review their armies. Comparison with Plate 12 reveals that the nineteenth-century engraver created more fanciful towers than actually existed. Allom 1870.

The common appellation used today—Forbidden City— captures well the seclusion afforded by the host of nested walls and mighty gates that isolated this sublime nucleus from the world outside. The Three Great Halls, Three Back Halls, Six Eastern Palaces and Six Western Palaces, an imperial garden, as well as other named palace complexes and courtyards, are an eloquent testament to Ming and Qing imperial design. Since this volume focuses on Beijing's walls and gates rather than on its palaces, space will not permit a review of the imposing assemblage of low but impressive structures that served the ceremonial, administrative, and residential requirements of the Son of Heaven. (A good accessible summary is Meyer 1991, 50–8.)

At the rear of the Forbidden City, where the wrapping walls converge, is Shenwumen (Gate of Divine Might) or, as it was once called, Xuanwumen (Gate of Occult Might). The lofty structure above the gateway contained drums and bells that would be sounded 108 times at dusk and dawn to mark time as the night passed. To the north of Shenwumen is a pyramid-shaped artificial hill that goes under various names, including Wanshoushan (Eternal Life Hill) during the Ming dynasty and Jingshan (Prospect Hill) during the Qing. It is also still commonly called Meishan (Coal Hill), since it long served as a storage space for the coal used for cooking and heating within the palace.

Just as Tiananmen, the Gate of Heavenly Peace, leads into the imperial city, so did Di'anmen, the Gate of Earthly Peace, once lead out of it to the north. Today, this complementary gate no longer stands. Beijing's axis continued northward to the Drum and Bell towers (Plate 14). The sequence of dark portals and open spaces—concealing and revealing—along the elongated 8-kilometre axis from the Yongding Gate to the Bell Tower augmented the sense of awe felt by those who traversed the full length. Daunting structures rising above the corners of the wall and imposing towers atop the gates afforded commoners a similar sense of amazement. The counterpoint of open space and structural mass, light and dark, horizontal lines punctuated by towers, as well as broad and restricted expanses, illustrate simplicity and grandeur simultaneously.

This linear geometrical order and its powerful architectural symbolism, whose origins reach deep into Chinese history, have been corrupted by a series of destructive measures taken throughout the twentieth century. The earliest changes in the form of Beijing's walls and gates emerged from episodic efforts at modernization, rather than any attack on the imperial past. As the power of the Qing dynasty waned and forces for innovation emerged at the end of the nineteenth century, practical necessity forced adjustments in the city's layout. The need for improved

4.8 Cleavages in the thick walls of Beijing in the early twentieth century were made to facilitate the introduction of steam railways into the city. Thomson 1913.

vehicular movement, in particular, led to the dismantling of the connecting walls of several gates. Ruptures were made into the formidable walls, as is seen in Figure 4.8, in order to permit steam locomotives to enter Beijing in the early part of the twentieth century.

Increasingly pervasive, however, were changes in intent in which 'imperial space' was transformed into 'people's space'. This transformation is best seen in the emergence of Tiananmen Square as a people's square, one that is today usually referred to as the 'heart of Beijing'. The largest public square in the world, with a purported capacity of more than half a million people, Tiananmen Square represents a level of openness that is in stark contrast with the impenetrable character of the nested walled spaces characteristic of imperial Beijing. Although Tiananmen 'the Gate' has a well-documented position in the symbolism of Beijing as a sacred city, Tiananmen 'the Square' has emerged only over the past half-century. Historic episodes in the twentieth century have drawn attention to the area immediately outside Tiananmen, the traditional nexus between China's rulers and its people; but Tiananmen Square's history is more recent. As Wu Hung (1991, 85) tells us, the emergence of the square 'provides a locus of coalescence for political expression, collective memory, identity, and history' for Chinese as well as non-Chinese.

Among the twentieth-century events associated with the Gate of Heavenly Peace are the demonstration on 4 May 1919 that protested the handing-over of Chinese territory to Japan by means of the Treaty of Versailles; the demonstration in December 1935 that crystallized resistance against Japanese aggression; the declaration of the founding of the People's Republic on 1 October 1949; the elaborate National Day parades held periodically afterwards, including the mass rallies during the Cultural Revolution of 1966 to 1976; and, finally and more recently, the student demonstrations and the infamous massacre in May and June 1989. Between 1919 and 1989, not only was there a reconfiguration of the spatial form of the area in front of Tiananmen and the placement and replacement of monuments and buildings, there was also a refashioning of the mental images of this critical location and other nearby and symbolically linked places.

After 1949, incremental changes altered the elongated T-shape that had developed during the imperial past. These alterations eventually brought forth a *guangchang* ('extensive open space') or plaza. The clearing of dilapidated *yamen* buildings adjacent to the T-shaped approach to Tiananmen created the first broadening of open space from that associated with the linear north/south axis. As this geometrical rupture occurred, the north/south axis was supplanted by a more prominent east/west axis along the route of broad Chang'an Boulevard, laid out to cross beneath Tiananmen. The creation of Tiananmen Square, as well as the socialist secular transformation of Beijing in general, was accompanied by the detachment of the Tiananmen from the axial and cosmological design of imperial times. Mao's use of Tiananmen as a rostrum for public spectacle placed it at a pivotal location at which the Chairman, like the emperors before him, looked south. Just as past emperors sat on their throne at a figurative central point from which power radiated and ritual originated, the Chairman, especially when representing the Red Sun during the frenzied pageants of the Cultural Revolution, similarly mediated with the public from a critical location via ritual. The 'square' took form as the expansive void came to be framed on four sides by dominating structures: the looming Gate of Heavenly Peace, the Great Hall of the People on the west, the Museum of Chinese History and Museum of the Chinese Revolution opposite, and the Mausoleum of Mao Zedong.

Even before the square had been completed, a decision was made to place a commemorative monument at a position some distance across the open area from Tiananmen (Plate 15). This 37 metre tall granite obelisk, completed in 1958, sits atop a storeyed plinth with ten marble relief sculptures that narrate the Chinese people's revolutionary struggle since 1849, beginning with the Opium War, resistance against the feudal order and imperialism, and finally civil war. Unlike any other structure on the traditional axis, this obelisk provides a juxtaposed dialectic relationship with the rostrum above the Tiananmen gate.

More so than the massive modern buildings on both sides of the square, this commemorative obelisk was viewed by sinophiles as an outrage against this great city. It appears as if this indeed was the intent of the post-1949 politicians and architects charged with reconstructing the new socialist capital. The building of this monument was 'an attempt to put a punctuation mark in the flow of history, to separate the past from the present' (Wu 1991, 100). Since 1976 and the death of Premier Zhou Enlai, the obelisk has become a place of protest in addition to that of memory, a tendency that culminated in 1989 in the student movement that emerged out of the commemoration of the death of Communist Party Secretary-General Hu Yaobang. The rapid construction of Mao's mausoleum in the year after his death in the autumn of 1976 further conspired to wrench away irretrievably whatever lingering signification there was in the historic longitudinal axis.

Alterations in Beijing's outer walls began during the Republican period, but demolition accelerated in the 1950s and was completed by 1962. This obliteration was accomplished ostensibly in order to create a ring road, a broad boulevard around the historic urban core, as well as to provide building materials for new construction projects. One might argue that the removal of the massive walls was the expected outcome of changing times, in which the city no longer required defensive bulwarks surrounding it. It must be remembered, however, that the walls of Beijing were maintained throughout the Ming and Qing dynasties less as a protective shield against some perceived threat than as the symbolic architecture of a great capital city. To the new rulers in Beijing, the walls indeed were seen as a graphic symbol, a geometric schematic, of a discredited imperial order. The elimination of Beijing's outer walls, through the Herculean efforts of Beijing's conscripted citizenry, had more to do with asserting a new socialist order with its contrary vision. Peculiarly, even though the walls came down relatively quickly, virtually all of Beijing's magnificent gates initially survived.

Beginning in 1966 with the first salvos of the Great Proletarian Cultural Revolution and lasting for the next decade, there was an orgy of devastation that was directed at the 'four olds'—thought, culture, customs, and habits—and the extirpation of all symbols of China's 'feudal past'. Besides city gates and other structures associated with the walls of China's old cities, many of the country's majestic historic sites, libraries, and museums, among other cultural resources, not only of Han culture but the work of ethnic minorities as well, were senselessly ravaged or destroyed. Much of this destruction was unheralded and not widely publicized, since foreigners were few in China during those years. When the Belgian sinologist Simon Leys returned to Beijing in 1972, he searched for several of the city's 'immortal' gates only to find them already reduced to rubble. 'Peking,' he declared, 'now appears to be a murdered town. The body is still there, the soul has gone.'

Several free-standing gates, corner towers, and the lines of the inner ring road around the city today merely suggest the scale and grandeur of imperial Beijing. Only the innermost crimson walls of the concentric plan remain, encircling the Imperial City and the Forbidden City, now heralded as the Palace Museum, a mere backdrop for the display of historic objects from China's feudal past. Even though most of the outer gates are no longer present, however, their resonant names of cosmological and historical symbolism continue to be used as markers of major subway and bus stations. They are but melancholy reminders of prominent sites of earlier times that have been substantially diminished by 'progress' and ideology.

Long before Beijing—and Chang'an as well—was an imperial capital, its material form pre-existed as a substantial idea pregnant with meaning. With many of the physical monuments and markers of China's imperial past now long gone, place names are still able to summon memories of times when an imperial capital was the pivot of the four quarters, the centre of a concentric world. The Chinese perceived Zhongguo, the Middle Kingdom, what we in the

West call China, as the centre of the world and its imperial capital at its metaphorical centre. This centring is all the more remarkable since neither Beijing nor Chang'an, nor any other Chinese imperial capital for that matter, is anywhere near the geographical centre of the empire.

5

Nanjing: Forgotten Grandeur

UPON THE DEMISE of Mongol Yuan rule, Zhu Yuanzhang, the rebel leader and founding emperor of the Ming dynasty, in 1368 established Nanjing as his capital. Situated in a region in which he had his power base but relatively far from the traditional northern capitals at Chang'an and Beijing, Nanjing became the first city south of the Yangtze to serve as the imperial seat of a unified China. Nanjing's tenure as an imperial capital under the Ming was short-lived and most of the city's grandeur has been erased over the centuries. Yet it is possible nonetheless to recall some of its glory from the last quarter of the fourteenth century and to see similarities and differences between it and the celebrated walled cities of Beijing and Chang'an.

In developing the design for building his capital on this topographically complex site, the Ming founder scripted a plan in which a sprawling settlement with irregularly shaped walls was protected by rivers and screened by mountains. This overall plan of an undulating outer wall differs significantly from the currently existing orthodox models, as well as from the geometrically regular plans of Tang Chang'an and the successor Ming capital at Beijing. F. W. Mote (1977, 113–14) reminds us, however, that 'a great capital incorporating both essentials from the whole tradition going back to Han and T'ang [Tang] times as well as elements of recent technological advances was quickly put together in a manner satisfactory to the despot who had just founded the new dynasty.' Commanding a strategic location, Nanjing occupied a hub position relative to water and land transport at a time of substantial economic development of the Yangtze basin. 'Accumulated historical associations', as Mote calls them, contributed to the 'royal air' that fortuitously elevated Nanjing's status as an imperial capital.

Zhu built a vast and impressive city that was expected to last for all time. When the rebel and pretender Zhu captured Nanjing in 1356, he acquired a modest walled city whose fortifications and layout included a former palace city of the Southern Tang dynasty (AD 937–75) that was being used as mere administrative offices for the prefecture it governed. By 1366, before he had vanquished the Mongols, Zhu had already begun the ambitious expansion of Nanjing's city walls beyond the existing perimeter, construction of a palace complex, and the building of shrines and altars needed by the emperor and his court. Although much of the work proceeded in piecemeal fashion, as new quarries and kilns were opened and artisans were recruited in increasing numbers, it is remarkable that the expanded city was essentially complete by 1373. Work continued until 1386, however, as is evidenced by dated bricks that have been excavated along the lines of the wall, providing evidence of the sequential completion of various sections. Well beyond the imposing city walls, a nearly circular and somewhat lower double set of earthen ramparts ringed the city.

Wrapped within a serpentine wall, whose line followed watercourses and irregular hills, Ming Nanjing included within it three districts: an imperial city with a walled palace city nested within it, the nearby city proper that included still-standing structures of earlier walled capitals, and a large open zone in the north-west (Fig. 5.1). The imperial precinct was located in the eastern part of the city. This relatively square precinct included an imperial city and a palace city that conformed to canonical geometrical conventions, boasting a well-defined axis, straight walls, symmetrically placed gates, a sequence of halls, and an age-old ordering of altars, temples, and shrines. Said to serve as the inspiration

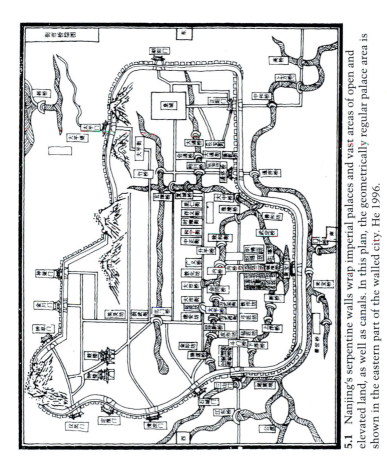

5.1 Nanjing's serpentine walls wrap imperial palaces and vast areas of open and elevated land, as well as canals. In this plan, the geometrically regular palace area is shown in the eastern part of the walled city. He 1996.

for the palaces later built by the Ming in Beijing, Nanjing's complex gradually fell into ruins, and by the beginning of the twentieth century there were only scant remains of the city's past glory.

Located to the west of the imperial precinct, in Ming times the city proper comprised commercial and residential areas. It is said that Zhu compelled some 20,000 wealthy families to build residences within the walls, an effort which contributed quickly to the transformation of Nanjing. The proliferation of textile, printing, and pottery workshops all drew upon the abundant resources of the Jiangnan region, a development dynamic that continued even after Nanjing ceased to be an imperial capital. Links between the inside and outside of the U-shaped walls that wrapped the city proper were facilitated by the presence of gates that led to the Qinhuai River. In addition, the Qinhuai, which served as part of the city's moat and was connected directly to a rich hinterland via the Yangtze, also had a branch that reached into the city via a sluice gate. Viewed as strategically important, the north-west portion of the city included vast irregular open tracts not suitable for building, as well as promontories that overlooked the approach to the Yangtze.

The building of Nanjing's walls set new standards for the extensive building and rebuilding of city walls throughout China. Ming walls were almost without exception qualitatively superior, as well as taller and broader, than those built in earlier dynasties (Plate 16). Nanjing's new walls were almost universally built on stone plinths, rather than on tamped-earth foundations, especially because much of the outer area was swampy and low. The transport of bulky stone and bricks was facilitated by the extensive network of watercourses that were threaded throughout the city. The unprecedented scale of city wall construction drew upon the resources of a large number of brickyards spread throughout the lower Yangtze region.

While tamped earth and rubble continued to provide the core for old and new walls, the use of fired bricks and stone slabs as facing far exceeded their utilization in the past. In Nanjing, each brick was stamped with the date and place of manufacture, as well as with the name of the brickmaker. This was done to insure quality: if the brick proved too fragile or deteriorated too quickly, the brickmaker was liable for its replacement. Brick facing was usually mortared with lime to stabilize the walls, which rose at least 12 metres above the ground. Capped with parapets, as is seen in Figure 5.2, the undulating wall beyond the built-up portions of the city is indeed reminiscent of the distant Great Wall. Along the southern section of the city's walls, some portions exceed 21 metres in height.

5.2   The parapets rising above the north-eastern section of Nanjing's walls are reminiscent of the Great Wall, as they snake along the ridges that overlook Purple Mountain in the distance. *Sketches of Nanking* 1933.

In addition to the generous scale of the walls, similar liberal treatments were given to moats and gates. The moats along the east, south, and west walls of Nanjing generally followed existing streams and ranged from 70 to 80 metres in width, although in some areas along the east side the width approached 200 metres. Thirteen gates were originally built, but this number was eventually increased to eighteen, with each surmounted by a multitiered tower. Since in Nanjing's case no wall was aligned precisely along a north/south meridian or an east/west parallel, individual gates themselves were not oriented to the cardinal directions.

Nanjing's walls were reinforced by a variety of *wengcheng*, in addition to a number of simple gates. All three of Nanjing's most imposing and dramatic *wengcheng* appear from the outside as mere portals, each with a low hole in the 16 metre high outer wall, and with crenellations and a large gate tower rising above it. However, as the view from the air seen in Figure 5.3 shows, the Tongji Gate along the southern wall was actually a formidable barbican that receded into the city rather than being attached to the outer wall. Visitors passed successively through four individual barrier-like gates and traverse a distance of 1.37 kilometres before actually entering the city. Over time and through periods of relative peace, much of the space within each one of the protective chambers became covered with low buildings that could be torched in case of an emergency.

Zhubao Gate, or Zhonghua Gate as it has been known in the twentieth century, was even more massive than was Tongji, rising three storeys and with an extensive system of tunnels within which soldiers were barracked. Between 1927 and 1937, when Nanjing served as the capital of the Republic of China, some fortified pillboxes were added along the top of the wall, but they subsequently proved ineffective in holding back the Japanese invaders. Sanshan Gate, located

5.3 The Tongji Gate was a complex barbican that actually included three additional walls to be passed before entry into the city could be achieved. Each of the open areas shown included barracks for soldiers. Zhu 1936.

on the west side of the city wall, had a massive set of four internal convex walls that were destroyed in December 1937 by Japanese bombs.

Nanjing's glory has alternated with periods of tragedy. Four hundred years ago, the Jesuit Matteo Ricci celebrated the city: 'In the judgment of the Chinese this city surpasses all other cities in the world in beauty and grandeur, and in this respect there are probably very few others superior or equal to it. . . . In some respects, it surpasses our European cities. . . . Though the king changed his residence to Pékin [Beijing] . . . Nankin [Nanjing] lost none of its splendor or its reputation.' After seeing Beijing, Ricci continued: 'The size of the city, the planning of its houses, the structure of its public buildings and its fortifications are far inferior to those of Nankin' (quoted in Mote 1977, 152–3).

The centuries that followed Ricci's comments sadly brought deterioration and neglect to Nanjing, especially to the grand imperial palaces that surpassed those still visible in Beijing. With the palaces destroyed by fire and their materials stolen to meet other needs, the few stone fragments that remain of Nanjing's past magnificence lie loosely scattered within the confines of a public park. Besides the impressive surviving city walls, only the Drum Tower, standing on a hill in the geographic centre of the walled city, remains as a prominent landmark of Nanjing's imperial grandeur.

Nanjing had a brief renaissance beginning in 1853, when the city served as the capital of the Taiping empire that contested Manchu rule. During this period, when Nanjing was renamed Tianjing (Heavenly Capital), new palaces, halls, gardens, and administrative buildings were constructed, but these too suffered devastation when imperial armies vanquished the Taiping Rebellion in 1864. Fires raged for three days and nights during the take-over and, although the massive walls largely survived, the flames produced a landscape of desolate ruins within the city.

When the new Nationalist government chose Nanjing to be the capital of the Republic of China in 1927, schemes were announced that would bring about the modernization of this ruined city. In the early part of the twentieth century, portions of the massive 14-metre thick southern wall had been dismantled in order to facilitate traffic in and out. A Western resident in the early 1930s wrote, 'A search for historical relics within Nanking [Nanjing] gives one a growing sense of wonder and of dismay, wonder at the richness and splendor of the past of this city, dismay that so little is known or remains. . . . Only here and there do we find a legend or a story, a monument and a battlefield, a name or a memorial, that, like stones on mountains containing ore, suggest the richness of the unfathomed mines beneath.' Under the Nationalists, wide boulevards for motorized traffic and new buildings for administration, commerce, and education concealed the scars of past tragedies, yet they also obscured most of the remaining vestiges of past imperial splendour. Within a decade, this progress was also arrested, devastated by the Japanese invasion of 1937.

Figure 5.4, showing part of the city walls' southern section, reveals clearly the fairly broad approach that passes over the moat, only to end at the constricted arch that allows passage through the wall. The maintenance of the gate tower and the central gate itself reveals some sensitivity to them as historic relics, while the nearby ruptures appear simply as a

5.4   In this view of a portion of the southern wall of Nanjing early in the twentieth century, the height and thickness of the wall dwarf the pedestrian traffic. Two ruptures in the wall facilitate movement even as the narrow central arch is being used. Zhu 1936.

utilitarian gesture. Chinese sources usually give various lengths for Nanjing's walls, but all agree that they were among the longest around any Chinese city. Although the commonly given figure is 50 kilometres, measurements taken from detailed air photographs of the city during the Second World War provide evidence for a figure closer to 37 kilometres (Mote 1977, 136). Today, some 21 kilometres remain in various states of repair. While the superiority of Nanjing's fortifications has often been proclaimed—the 'highest, longest, widest, firmest, and most impressive city wall in China' (Mote 1977, 134)—so too has Beijing been highlighted and marked as the 'the ultimate achievement in Chinese imperial city planning' (Steinhardt 1990, 166). Which is the quintessential Chinese imperial walled city is, indeed, impossible to resolve. Like the Great Wall that rises and falls along the rugged mountain ranges of China's periphery, inspiring awe in all those who gaze upon it, the magnificent still-standing walls and gates of Nanjing continue to be a source of wonder. As the century ends, regrettably, only Beijing—alone rather than together with Nanjing—is still able to convey a sense of the palpable grandeur and symbolic gravity of China's imperial building tradition.

6

Pingyao: Old China Preserved

THE TWENTIETH-CENTURY TRANSFORMATIONS of Beijing, Nanjing, and Xi'an have obscured the historic walls, gates, and other structures left over from the imperial pasts associated with these great cities. What artefacts still stand in these and other major Chinese cities, towns, and villages jostle with modern elements to the degree that there is a diminishing of any distinct sense of place, whether old or new. While there are still some walled settlements throughout the countryside that evoke Chinese life in past centuries, it is difficult to find any sentiments of antiquity in most of China's rapidly changing cities and towns. Post-1949 urban development has generally ravaged historic sites throughout the country, eradicating substantial elements of the cultural fabric that gave each locale its distinct sense of place.

While individual monuments and somewhat more extensive historic districts indeed have been preserved in some cities, it is rare to find a large urban settlement that has not been overwhelmed by the forces of twentieth-century social and economic changes. Arguably, the single outstanding exception to this generalization is the little-known city of Pingyao in the central plateau of Shanxi province, some 90 kilometres south of the provincial capital, Taiyuan. Pingyao today is a relatively small town with a population of only 47,000 and a total area of 4.2 square kilometres, but its dramatic walls and quiet lanes suggest that it was once a more important walled city (Fig. 6.1).

With its imposing crennelated brick walls that surround a low-rise cityscape of old buildings, Pingyao evokes 'old China' (Plate 17). While the city is no living fossil, untouched by the unsightly intrusion of industrialization and

6.1 The grand battered walls of Pingyao with their projecting terraces rise from the parched tawny soils that are characteristic of central Shanxi province.

uncontrolled urban growth, it is remarkably free of the sweeping destruction common in better-known cities. Taiyuan, for example, has swelled in size over the past half-century as a result of industrialization fueled by abundant natural resources. Taiyuan's 11 kilometre long walls, as well as its temples and monuments, were all gradually destroyed, so that little of historic significance remains within the city, a development that has repeated itself throughout China. Several magnificent temples, however, still stand in the suburbs of Taiyuan and suggest the architectural grandeur of Shanxi province in times past.

After the founding of the People's Republic in 1949, Pingyao and a few other small cities fortunately slipped into a state of relative obscurity that slowed the pace of destruction. Several other smaller Shanxi cities besides Pingyao—such as Taigu, Xinfeng, and Jiexiu—also still had their outer walls in the 1960s. Little by little, however, their walls were demolished, so that by the end of the 1970s, as Deng Xiaoping's new policies unleashed a torrent of construction in China, only the walls of Pingyao remained. They too were slated for belated removal, as a lack of maintenance over the years had taken its toll and significant portions of the walls had become dangerously dilapidated. In the summer of 1977, however, when Pingyao was seriously threatened by flooding and it was the presence of the walls, functioning as a levee, that saved the city, many began to question the wisdom of removing them.

Another danger came in 1981 when experts, who had been invited to carry out a master plan for the nearby city of Yuci, recommended the massive 'modernization' of Pingyao. The proposed plan would significantly impact the city's walls: it included the laying-out of broad roads within Pingyao, as well as the renewal of districts with old residences, and the rupturing of the wall in eight locations in order to open the city to the surrounding countryside. Removal of the eastern walls and old residences began almost immediately, but because of successful appeals to the provincial and national governments for restraint, a new master plan for salvaging Pingyao's integrity was initiated in time to subvert the planned 'rejuvenation' of the city.

This success was made possible by an extraordinary confluence of civic boosterism, professional historic preservation, bureaucratic initiative, and good fortune that thwarted the removal of Pingyao's signature walls. In the nearly two decades since, preservation work has continued apace to restore much of the city to its former glory. In 1997, Pingyao joined a host of better-known Chinese cultural and natural sites in being declared a World Heritage Site by UNESCO, the only Chinese common-walled city to have this status.

With this as background, what are the essential elements that elevated Pingyao to a rank equalled by no other non-imperial Chinese city? Mere survival is an obvious reason.

Over the centuries, certainly a very large number of grand walled cities were constructed throughout China, most of which were never visited, photographed, or evaluated by Westerners. Many such walled cities did not survive changes in dynasties over the ages, falling into disrepair as their fortunes waned. Furthermore, few city walls have been valued as monuments in and of themselves. As was discussed in the previous chapter, even the grandeur of the walled imperial capital of Nanjing, constructed in the fourteenth century, was eclipsed quickly as Beijing's prominence rose and architectural superlatives were attached to it alone. There indeed may have been more beautiful, more complete, and more significant Chinese walled cities, but it is Pingyao that has survived relatively intact. It offers concrete evidence of the historic scale and imposing form of walled cities that were not imperial capitals.

The walls seen today of the 'ancient city', as Pingyao is commonly called, were actually only built at the beginning of the Ming dynasty in 1370. During the early years of the Ming, existing tamped-earth walls were reinforced, faced with fired brick, and expanded as well. Over the centuries, watch-towers, gate towers, and improved battlements were constructed, sometimes in response to an imperial inspection tour by a Ming or Qing emperor. Pingyao's walls are essentially square, with a perimeter of approximately 6.2 kilometres and ringed by a moat from which much of the earth for the rising wall was obtained. The wall's foundation is an elevated tamped podium, with the core of the wall itself also composed of rammed earth. The 10 metre high walls are battered, that is, gradually sloping from the base to the top, and faced with fired brick. At the base, the walls' width ranges from 9 to 12 metres, while at the top it is between 3 and 6 metres. The top has been paved with bricks in order to drain off rainwater (Plate 18). Except for the wavy southern wall, which follows the bank of the Fen River, the walls are straight.

Distinctive features of the profile of Pingyao are the 71 terraced embattlements that stand about 50 metres apart and the roughly 3,000 crenels, indented openings that are wider on the inside than on the outside, that give the parapet the look of a gigantic saw on edge. The terraced projecting embattlements, which also contained guardhouses, are called *mamian* ('horse faces'), in order to designate the prominently protruding parts of the wall that would overpower any intruders who would approach it (Fig. 6.2).

On each of the four corners was a large watch-tower constructed of wooden columns and beams. Six gate towers were mounted on the walls, two on each of the side walls and one on both the north and south walls. Common lore tells that the gate towers and watch-towers were destroyed during the Japanese occupation of the area after 1938. Only one, Kuixing Tower, has been reconstructed, but there are

6.2 One of seventy-two structures that sit astride a projecting terrace, this served in the past as a guardhouse and residence for several soldiers.

plans to rebuild several others. Each of the six gates was buttressed with a *wengcheng*, either in a protruding form or simply with a double gate, whose purpose was to reinforce the gate in the surface of the wall.

This configuration of six gates has contributed to a view of the city as shaped like a tortoise, a form that symbolizes longevity (Fig. 6.3). The four east and west gates are said to represent the tortoise's four legs. Three of the *wengcheng* have outer gate openings towards the south and are said to represent the forward motion of the tortoise. The north-eastern gate, opening towards the east, is believed to be tethered to the Lutai Pagoda that is some 10 kilometres away. The northern gate, which is situated in a low-lying area and through which the rainwater and sewage are drained, is viewed as the tail and anus of the city. The southern gate is said to be the tortoise's head and leads directly to a water source. Two wells outside the southern gate traditionally were seen as the eyes. The tortoise shape is clearly apparent

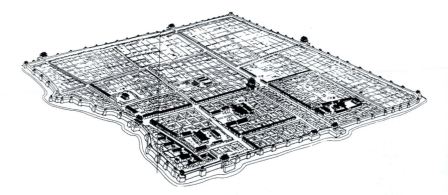

6.3 This perspective drawing highlights the regularity of three sides of Pingyao and the irregularity of its southern wall. The curving line on the left is said to represent the front shoulder of a tortoise, with strategically positioned gates indicating the location of its head, feet, and tail.

when viewing the city's shape from the air, as its form sprawls across the khaki-coloured ground, but it is remarkable that those who never viewed the shape from above were able to imagine it this way.

Entering the city from either of the gates on the western side, one comes first to a kind of holding chamber in the projecting *wengcheng* that leads to a second gate set directly into the wall. Once inside, there are steps and ramps that lead up to the parapeted upper surface of the elevated wall, from which it is easy to view the city's low skyline. What one sees are low tawny buildings with their high backs, single-sloped roofs, and surrounding walls that are representative examples of Shanxi and Shaanxi vernacular architectural forms. In the distance is a three-storey, 18.5 metre high wooden structure called a *shilou* (market tower) (Fig. 6.4). Built in Qing style with a double-eaved roof

6.4 Most of the buildings remaining within Pingyao are residences and shops. At the center of the walled city is the Market Tower.

supported by bracket arms, the structure actually straddles the main thoroughfare that arrives from the southern gate and served as a drum tower.

Compared to other Chinese towns, Pingyao lacks colour and activity. Bicycles and motorbikes, pedestrians and carts, dominate the narrow lanes, although the numbers of vehicles seen are also increasing. The occasional truck or bus is frustrated as it attempts to travel lanes laid out centuries ago to accommodate humans and animals alone.

Walking along Pingyao's dusty lanes, one encounters a maze-like warren that is punctuated by grand gates that lead through walls into narrow residential courtyards. Traditionally, Pingyao's residences were built to mimic the cave-like dwellings that are still commonly seen elsewhere in that loessial region where wood is rare. Here, however, the expressions of the wealth of those residing in those dwellings are generously framed and ornamented with wood.

As one gets closer to the Market Tower, near the geographical centre of Pingyao, it becomes clear what the base of wealth was for this quiet town. Rather than commodities or industry, Pingyao's wealth historically derived from banking! Efforts are now being made to restore the financial core of Pingyao that revolved around an institution called the *piaohao*. In the early part of the eighteenth century, commerce throughout China was in the hands of traders from three areas: southern Anhui, central Shanxi, and southern Fujian. Those from Shanxi, including the Pingyao area, created a remittance banking system, a vital component of long-distance, countrywide commerce. In the mid-nineteenth century, the country's commerce began to focus more on the coastal rim, relying on modern banks such as those based in Ningbo, Zhejiang province. Until the rise of the Ningbo bankers, who eclipsed their Pingyao counterparts in the early twentieth century, the

Shanxi *piaohao* monopolized finance and business transactions throughout China.

Near the city's commercial core and in the shadow of the Market Tower, several of the seven original *piaohao* in Pingyao are being restored as museums of the city's distinctive commercial history. Displays detail how competing *piaohao* issued convertible paper notes or remittance certificates that could be carried more easily than bulky bars of silver or strings of coins. The inability of the weakened Qing imperial system to implement a modern currency and banking system created a vacuum that was filled by the creative *piaohao* money traders, who established branch offices in China's major coastal and riverine commercial cities. The most celebrated *piaohao* were housed in sumptuous wooden structures that open to the street like any other shop and have impressive names, such as 'The Rising Sun Brings Prosperity Piaohao' and 'One Hundred Rivers Flow Together Piaohao'. The enterprise of the Shanxi bankers throughout the nineteenth century brought substantial wealth to the Pingyao region, prosperity that is reflected in the extensive commercial buildings and fine dwellings found everywhere within the city's walls.

Pingyao was once filled with some forty impressive temples, as well as other buildings serving its civil administration. Virtually all these buildings, like the city itself, faced south. Most are now gone, but the magnificence of the city's walls and its internal structures are mirrored in the extraordinary walled estates that still dot the surrounding countryside. Together they demonstrate the now lost prosperity of central Shanxi in times past. Over the past fifty years, these embarrassing emblems of indigenous capitalism were rarely noted, and they were certainly not visited by Chinese or foreign visitors. That the buildings have survived is a testament to those living in central Shanxi, who preserved these unique and unusual architectural forms, protecting tangible expressions of the region's commercial prominence and the eminence of individual families.

Perhaps the most outstanding walled compound or estate in the countryside outside of Pingyao is that known as the Qiaojia Dayuan (the Qiao family manor). In order to meet the needs of a large and growing extended household in the nineteenth century, the Qiao manor complex eventually came to comprise six major courtyard compounds with some twenty smaller courtyards that cover an area of 8,700 square metres. The Qiao family flourished from trading activities centred at Xikou, now called Baotou, beyond the Great Wall in what is today Inner Mongolia. Specializing in trade in pigments, flour, grain, and oils, as well as running several pawnshops, they eventually expanded their business far beyond the borders of northern China and by the end of the nineteenth century operated coal mines, specialized shops, and an extensive banking network. The Qing Empress Cixi stopped at the Qiao family estate in the summer of 1900, at the close of the Boxer Uprising, as she fled with the young emperor to Xi'an in the wake of the arrival in Beijing of an international expeditionary force.

Changes in the national economy in the first decades of the twentieth century reduced the family's income and, according to popular beliefs, the profligacy of the fifth generation descendants of the clan's founder led to the bankruptcy of the clan. By the early 1930s, the family had divided its assets and the manor fell into disrepair, finally being abandoned after the Japanese invasion in 1937. After 1949 the complex was taken over by local authorities, who used it as an army barracks as well as for other governmental functions. Substantial destruction occurred during the Cultural Revolution. In 1985, the manor's fortunes, if not those of the clan, turned again, as the complex was designated a museum with substantial funds apportioned for its repair. The grandeur of the Qiao family's estate and its many walls and gates are apparent to viewers of Zhang Yimou's 1991 film, *Raise the Red Lantern*. Zhang's story is one of deceit, treachery, and sexual favours in a wealthy Chinese clan at the beginning of the twentieth century—all occurring within the confines of a grand feudal mansion. His tale, however, is not that of the Qiao family, the story of whose rise and fall is itself worthy of being told.

The Qiao family estate is a walled city in miniature that echoes well the nested structure of walls-within-walls characteristic of Chinese walled cities. The walls not only portray the need to delineate property and provide security, they also reflect the level of prosperity in this relatively remote and apparently poor area. Throughout Shanxi today, there is optimism that the historical walled compounds that remain will contribute to the resurgence of the region's prestige and fame, as people throughout China and the world are made aware of its past commercial glory. The designation of the walls surrounding Pingyao as a world-class monument, as well as the opening of a modern expressway between Taiyuan and Beijing, cutting travel time in half to six hours, are expected to insure this rise in recognition of the region's past eminence and future promise. Seeing Pingyao as 'China's banking capital', even for a relatively short period, helps to clarify why the city is so securely wrapped within its prominent walls.

Destruction and Preservation of a Legacy

FINDING WAYS to maintain a city's architectural heritage while carrying out modernization is a monumental and difficult set of tasks. Indeed, throughout the world urban landscapes and historic structures from the past have been ravaged by 'progress', and it is as exceptional for preservation to dominate over destruction in Asia as it has been in the Americas and Europe. Moreover, preservation successes all too often have come about fitfully and accidentally, so that what does survive from the past is usually disfigured, decontextualized, and merely suggestive of earlier forms. It has been more likely for an individual building to be preserved than a cluster of buildings, more likely that a structure be recycled that can serve a new purpose than one that appears to have outlived its usefulness. Fortifications—such as city walls—that were necessary in times past have generally been seen as impediments to progress because of their sheer size and the magnitude of the areas they occupy.

All over the world, massive city walls and gates have been readily sacrificed, leaving only faint and sometimes ill-defined traces of their lapsed significance. Contemporary maps of cities in Europe and America frequently hint at the outlines of early walls in the layout and internal arrangement of the contemporary urban spaces. Names of places especially preserve the memory of gates and towers that once dominated specific areas, even when no one can recall any longer their original form. Wall Street in New York City, to take one example, was once the location of a palisaded line of fortifications surrounding the Dutch settlement of New Amsterdam, but it is today delineated only by the tall buildings along it. The French word *boulevard* once described the top surface of a city wall, then the encircling roadway that was laid out along its demolished line, before entering common usage as a spacious tree-lined promenade whose link to ancient ramparts is no longer appreciated. In some places in Europe where old gates are preserved, they sometimes form the impressive core of a circle that shapes a geometry of traffic flow quite different from that of early times. It is perhaps expecting too much that China would be any more protective of the physical remains of its historical walled cities than has been true elsewhere in the world.

Over several thousand years, Chinese city wall construction, destruction, and reconstruction have gone through prominent cycles well noted in the historical records. Over the past century, age, neglect, warfare, and policy have conspired to obliterate the physical remains of walls that once were thought to be indestructible. Sometimes it was the lack of preventative maintenance of aging structures and simple neglect that led to cracking and crumbling, as gravity and weather lowered profiles and ravished seemingly hardened surfaces. Other massive walls were destroyed slowly over long periods during peaceful times because peasants reclaimed the pounded soil in order to refashion fields and hillsides for farming or 'borrowed' bricks to build their dwellings. From time to time, dismantling and destruction arose from bureaucratic decisions, as bricks and earth were removed and used for other purposes.

Over the past two centuries, warfare has shattered seemingly impregnable fortresses in China by the introduction of Western weaponry, first from bombardment at ground level and then, during the Second Sino-Japanese War in the 1930s, from the air. As is seen in several of the photographs, several times during the twentieth century there have been episodes of partial destruction, such as the cutting through of walls in order to give access to railroads, as China carried forth its modernization after the Revolution of 1911. Each time a wall was partially breached to facilitate the laying of a railroad or road, it was inevitable that nearby sections also would fall.

In Taipei, where the city walls were destroyed during the Japanese occupation early in the twentieth century, a handful of gates survived as the centre-pieces of traffic circles. Even as recently as 1966, as is seen in Plate 4, each surviving gate was able to dominate its circle, since the scale of the surrounding buildings and the volume of traffic was minimal. Today, however, some of these gates have been overwhelmed by Brobdingnagian elevated roadways that soar about them and changing traffic patterns that impinge upon their scale (Plate 19). In more recent times, on the Mainland wholesale obliteration of traditional massive walls around towns and cities occurred at an accelerating rate, as New China turned its back on the nation's imperial past in an effort to modernize quickly.

After 1949, weighty structures as well as more fragile traditional buildings, such as temples, bell towers, altars, gates, honorific arches, and towers, among many other markers of imperial geometry, were summarily destroyed, abandoned, or given over to alternative uses on an unprecedented scale in an attempt to obliterate China's imperial, now called 'feudal', patrimony. Inevitably, the meanings and functions of surviving buildings were turned inside out, as one by one they became factories, barracks, or schools.

The redesign of Beijing as the new capital of the People's Republic of China led in particular to the regrettable destruction of the city's magnificent walls and gates, as did similar levelling around other cities in order to meet the needs of expanding populations and the exigencies of transport improvement. Many have judged these losses over the years to be not only regrettable but also irredeemable. It is thus remarkable that recent years have seen some significant attempts to repair the tattered fabric of traditional walled urban forms and to uncover even the ruins of forms that have been preserved simply because they were buried. Chinese newspapers regularly report on these efforts, with optimists buoyed and pessimists continuing to despair, since destruction continues apace. It is an incontrovertible fact that the Chinese public at large is generally unsentimental about the loss of traditional architecture, viewing demolition— perhaps even the erosion of traditional culture in general—as the necessary, if unfortunate, accompaniment to progress.

On the other hand, archaeological excavation reports, conservation and restoration programs, technological breakthroughs, and incipient grass-roots awareness of the value of China's architectural heritage are noteworthy positive elements that must be acknowledged. Today, images snatched by orbiting satellites sketch for those who are interested the lines of phantom-like walls of former imperial capitals, whose terrestrial existence is not clearly apparent on the ground. Aerial photography, remote sensing, and computerized enhancement in recent years have helped establish mappable details of ancient cities that supplement literary and archaeological findings for scholars.

News reports of 'city ruins discovered' provide provinces with opportunities to vie for who has the earliest city walls; each discovery seems to push back the dates of China's urban history. Among the 'earliest city ruins' and details concerning 'ancient city relics' announced in various recent press reports are:

walls and moats that date back 6,000 years discovered in Chengtoushan, Hunan province;

circular walls, with some 290 metres still intact, of a neolithic 'city' dated 4,800–5,300 years ago and discovered near Xishan, Zhengzhou, Henan province;

2.3 metre high rammed-earth walls, 14 metres wide at the top and 19 metres at the bottom, with a moat, in Yanshi, Henan province, dated to the Shang period (c.1700–1100 BC);

a five-sided wall that covers an area of 320,000 square metres at Zhishu, Sichuan province;

and other very early city remains in Xinjin, Pixian, and Dujiangyan, Sichuan province.

In addition, a major Tang-period city, possibly modelled after Chang'an, has been discovered at Yangzhou, Jiangsu province. The town includes intersecting thoroughfares running 3.5 kilometres from east to west and 5.5 kilometres from north to south and covered an area of 18.8 square kilometres.

Using remote-sensing technology, it has been determined that Tang Chang'an covered an area of 34.39 square kilometres and was wrapped by 25 kilometre long city walls. Remote sensing has also been used to delineate the nested fortifications of Khubilai Khan's thirteenth-century Shangdu (or Xanadu as it was called by Marco Polo). The square outer walls have been shown to have been 8.5 kilometres long. Original street patterns and even shop building lots that had not been observable on the ground have been delimited using aerial photography.

South-west of today's Beijing, the drainage system beneath the southern wall of Zhongdu, the Liao and Jin capital of the tenth to thirteenth centuries, is now housed in a museum of 'ancient city ruins'. And in Beijing itself, the walls around the imperial city and the palace city are being rebuilt and refaced in order to shore up sections that had crumbled because of wind and rain damage.

Each of these, however, is an essentially disconnected effort that exposes the reality that comprehensive national, provincial, and local measures are poorly developed and sorely needed. There is no substitution for such a concerted action, though the piecemeal efforts seen thus far have been surprisingly effective.

During the demolition of some old buildings in Beijing in September 1996, a remnant core section of the Ming-dynasty wall that was only 100 metres long and less than 6 metres high was uncovered. Some of the bricks were clearly incised with characters indicating that they had been made in 1541. News of this discovery in the local newspapers sparked a great deal of interest and within a month a decision was made to rebuild this precious short section of the wall and to develop a city wall museum on an adjacent site. The Beijing Cultural Relics Bureau reached out to city residents, urging them to cooperate by donating relic bricks that they might have obtained when the walls were dismantled in the 1960s. Weighing some 24 kilograms and measuring 48 centimetres long, 24 centimetres wide, and 12 centimetres thick, an unknown number of these crude gray bricks indeed had been rescued as treasures by countless numbers of city dwellers. Although representing but a fraction of the total number of bricks in the original city wall, some 60,000 individual bricks had already been obtained by November 1997, and there were hopes that at least 200,000 more would come to light in the coming years. While this nominal reconstruction was taking place, some 52 kilometres south of Beijing in Hebei province, work was underway to reproduce Beijing's historic walls and gate towers as part of a large-scale tourist attraction (Fig. 7.1).

Attention in recent years has turned to reclaiming and reconstructing remnants of what continues to be labelled, paradoxically, 'artefacts from the feudal past' as respectable tourist attractions. In addition, new 'old' walled cities are being planned and constructed to meet the needs of China's burgeoning tourist business. Whatever remains, however, is rarely contextualized, surviving simply as 'potted landscapes'

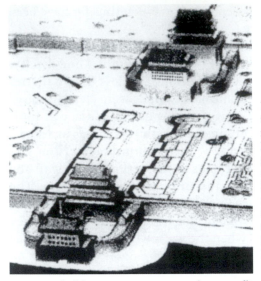

7.1 For purposes of tourism and historical nostalgia, some of Beijing's walls and gates are being recreated some 52 kilometres away from the Ming and Qing imperial capital amid the tawny fields of Hebei province. China Daily, 20 October 1992.

surrounded by new structures that conflict with the old ones. Each surviving structure normally represents nothing more than an isolated fragment of a grand, organized, and unified material tapestry, whose complex meaning once transcended the tamped earth, fired brick, stone, and wood with which they were composed. Throughout China, in old imperial capitals and provincial towns, some few voices are speaking up for rebuilding structures that are no longer standing and for recreating past streetscapes. As international and domestic tourism to China has increased, planners and others concerned with the maintenance and/or presentation of traditional Chinese culture have called for historic preservation and even restoration of the country's city walls. In doing so, they have underscored the fact that those walls— whether imperial or more plebian—are more than archaeological relics. They are important expressions of Chinese monumental architecture and a tangible statement of traditional cultural values that link humans with the cosmos.

Selected Bibliography

Bishop, Carl Whiting (1938), 'An Ancient Chinese Capital: Earthworks at Old Ch'ang-an,' *Antiquity: A Quarterly Journal of Archaelogy*, 12: 68–78.

Chang, Sen-dou (1961), 'Some Aspects of the Urban Geography of the Chinese Hsien Capital,' *Annals of the Association of American Geographers*, 51(1): 23–45.

—— (1970), 'Some Observations on the Morphology of Chinese Walled Cities,' *Annals of the Association of American Geographers*, 60(1): 63–91.

—— (1977), 'The Morphology of Walled Capitals,' In G. W. Skinner, ed., *The City in Late Imperial China*, Stanford: Stanford University Press.

Chiang, Tao-chang (1980), 'Walled Cities and Towns in Taiwan,' in Ronald G. Knapp, ed., *China's Island Frontier: Studies in the Historical Geography of Taiwan*, Honolulu: University of Hawai'i Press.

Davidson, James N. (1903), *The Island of Formosa*, Yokohama: Kelly & Walsh, Ltd.

Du Halde, Jean Baptiste (1736), *Description geographique, historique, chronologique, politique, et physique de l'empire de la Chine et de la Tartarie chinoise*, Paris: Henri Scheurleer.

Gaubatz, Piper Rae (1996), *Beyond the Great Wall: Urban Form and Transformation on the Chinese Frontiers*, Stanford: Stanford University Press.

Hommel, Rudolf P. (1937), *China at Work: An Illustrated Record of the Primitive Industries of China's Masses, Whose Life Is Toil, and Thus an Account of Chinese Civilization*, New York: John Day Co.

Hou Renzhi (1986), 'The Transformation of the Old City of Beijing, China,' in Michael P. Conzen, ed., *World*

Patterns of Modern Urban Change: Essays in Honor of Chauncey D. Harris, Chicago: University of Chicago, Department of Geography Research Paper, Nos. 217–18.

Ishiwari Heizō (1940), *Shina Jōkaku no Gaiyō* [General outline of the walled cities of China], Tokyo: Japanese Expeditionary Forces in China.

Knapp, Ronald G. (1980), 'Walled Cities: Knots in a Cosmic Landscape,' *Orientations*, 11(11): 43–9.

—— (1999), *China's Living Houses: Folk Beliefs, Symbols, and Household Ornamentation*, Honolulu: University of Hawai'i Press.

—— (2000), *China's Old Dwellings*, Honolulu: University of Hawai'i Press.

Lamley, Harry J. (1977), 'The Formation of Cities: Initiative and Motivation in Building Three Walled Cities in Taiwan,' in G. W. Skinner, ed., *The City in Late Imperial China*, Stanford: Stanford University Press.

Liu, Cary Y. (1992), 'The Yüan Dynasty Capital, Ta-tu: Imperial Building Program and Bureaucracy,' *T'oung Pao*, 78: 264–301.

Meyer, Jeffrey F. (1978), 'Feng-shui of the Chinese City,' *History of Religions*, 18: 138–55.

—— (1991), *The Dragons of Tiananmen: Beijing as a Sacred City*, Columbia: University of South Carolina Press.

Mote, F. W. (1974), 'A Milennium of Chinese Urban History: Form, Time, and Space Concepts in Soochow,' *Rice University Studies*, 59(4): 35–65.

—— (1977), 'The Transformation of Nanking, 1350–1400,' in G. W. Skinner, ed., *The City in Late Imperial China*, Stanford: Stanford University Press.

Needham, Joseph (1971), *Science and Civilisation in China*, Vol. 4, Pt. 3, London: Cambridge University Press.

Schinz, Alfred (1996), *The Magic Square: Cities in Ancient China*, Stuttgart and London: Edition Axel Menges.

Siren, Osvald (1924), *Walls and Gates of Peking*, London: John Lane.

Steinhardt, Nancy Shatzman (1990), *Chinese Imperial City Planning*, Honolulu: University of Hawai'i Press.

———— (1998), 'Mapping the Chinese City: The Image and the Reality,' in David Buisseret, ed., *Envisioning the City: Six Studies in Urban Cartography*, Chicago: University of Chicago Press.

———— (1983), 'The Plan of Khubilai Khan's Imperial City,' *Artibus Asiae* 44(2/3): 137–58.

———— (1986), 'Why Were Chang'an and Beijing So Different?,' *Journal of the Society of Architectural Historians*, 45: 339–57.

Waley, Arthur, trans. (1937), *The Book of Songs*, London: G. Allen & Unwin.

Wallacker, Benjamin E., Ronald G. Knapp, Arthur J. Van Alstyne, and Richard J. Smith, eds. (1979), *Chinese Walled Cities: A Collection of Maps from Shina Jôkaku no Gaiyô*, Hong Kong: Chinese University of Hong Kong Press.

Wheatley, Paul (1971), *The Pivot of the Four Quarters: A Preliminary Inquiry into the Origins and Character of the Ancient Chinese City*, Chicago: Aldine Publishing Co.

Wright, Arthur F. (1977), 'The Cosmology of the Chinese City,' in G. W. Skinner, ed., *The City in Late Imperial China*, Stanford: Stanford University Press.

———— (1965), 'Symbolism and Function: Reflections on Changan [Chang'an] and Other Great Cities,' *Journal of Asian Studies*, 24(4): 667–79.

Wu Hung (1991), 'Tiananmen Square: A Political History of Monuments,' *Representations*, 35: 84–117.

Xu Yinong (1994), 'The City as a Sacred Cosmos: Symbolism in the Construction of Wu and Yue Capitals,' *Edinburgh Architecture Research*, Vol. 21: 24–49.

—— (1996), *The City in Space and Time: Development of the Urban Form and Space of Suzhou until 1911*, Unpublished Ph.D. dissertation, University of Edinburgh.

Index

Administrative functions of walled
cities, 38
Anhui, 94
Archaeological evidence, 15–16,
101–102

Banpo neolithic site, 50
Barbicans, 30–31, 82, 83, 85
Beijing (Ming and Qing capital), 13,
19, 21, 27, 28, 39, 41, 43–45,
53–76, 86, 87, 100, 102–104,
105
Beiping (Ming capital), 57
Bell and Drum Towers, 36–38, 50,
51, 59, 70, 84
Bishop, Carl Whiting, 18–19
Brick-faced walls, 15, 19, 20–22,
80–82, 90–91, 103

Chang, Sen-dou, 4
Chang'an (Han and Tang capitals),
13, 18–19, 38, 42–52
Chengdu, Sichuan, 31
Contemporary cities, 1
Corner towers, 2, 27–41, 61, 75,
91–92

Dadu (Yuan capital), 53–58
Dali, Yunnan, 22
Darning Gong, 48
Daxing (Sui capital), 46, 48, 51
Defense and the building of walled
cities, 7–9, 31, 32, 64–65, 82, 83
Defensive projections (mamien
and wengcheng), 31, 32, 64–65,
82, 83, 88, 91–92, 93
Dingxian, Hebei, 29, 30
Du Halde, J. B., 63–64

Embankments against flooding,
5–6
Enceinte, 30–32, 43
External morphology of walled
cities, 11–15

Fengshui and the siting of walled
cities, 9–11, 40
Forbidden City (Beijing), 64, 67–70,
75
Foundations, 22–24, 80–81
Fujian, 5, 6, 13, 14, 15, 24, 94

Ganzhou, Jiangxi, 5, 33
Gate towers, 64, 67–70, 85
Gates, 5, 27–41, 43, 46, 55–56, 62,
75, 82, 92–93
Geomancy, see Fengshui
Great Proletarian Cultural
Revolution, 73, 74–75, 96
Great Wall, 1, 16, 96
Guangdong,15, 24, 31, 32
Guangzhou, Guangdong, 31, 32

Han dynasty walled cities, 20, 31,
36, 42–43, 46, 49, 50, 77
Hangtu (tamped earth
construction), 15–27
Hangzhou, Zhejiang, 14
Hebei, 29, 30, 35, 39, 103
Heian-kyō, Japan, 49
Henan, 35, 101
Historic preservation issues, 88–
89, 98–104
Hommel, Rudolf, 29
Huai'an, Jiangsu, 5
Hunan, 101

Imperial way, 63, 65, 71–72
Internal form of walled cities,
33–41, 60–71, 92–95
Ishiwari Heizō, 13, 30, 31, 35

Jiangnan, 31–32
Jiangsu, 10, 23, 27, 30, 32, 102
Jiangxi, 14, 15, 24, 33

Kaifeng, Henan, 6, 21, 27
Kaogong ji, 12, 45, 47, 54–55
Kessel, Dmitri, 67
Khubilai Khan, 54, 57, 102
Kyongju, Korea, 49

Leys, Simon, 75

Mamien (defensive projections), 88, 91–92
Mancheng, Hebei, 27
Manchus, 2, 41, 51–52, 61–64
Markets, 37, 47, 93–95
Ming dynasty walled cities, 2, 15, 20, 42, 45, 50, 57–65, 77–86, 90
Moats, 5, 6, 15, 21, 26–27, 55–56, 82
Mongols, 53–58, 62, 77–78
Mote, F. W., 77, 83, 86

Nanjing, Jiangsu (Ming capital), 23, 27, 77–86, 87, 90
Needham, Joseph, 11–12

Parapets, 21–22, 61, 62, 81
Pingyao, Shanxi, 13, 87–97

Qiaojia Dayuan (Qiao family manor), 96–97
Qin dynasty walled cities, 16, 42, 50
Qinding gujin tushu jicheng (imperial encyclopedia), 2
Qing dynasty walled cities, 15, 41, 43, 45, 50–51, 59, 63–65, 84, 93
Quanzhou, Fujian, 5, 6

Republican period walled cities, 2, 74, 82–84
Ricci, Matteo, 83–84
Riverbanks as preferred sites for walled cities, 4–7
Round walled cities, 13–14

Shaanxi, 49–52, 93
Shandong, 35
Shang dynasty, 102
Shanghai, 13–14
Shanxi, 33, 34, 35, 87–97
Shaoxing, Zhejiang, 14
Shijing (Book of Songs), 16–17
Shuimen (water gates), 31–32
Sichuan, 8, 31, 102
Site preferences for walled cities, 3–9

Song dynasty walled cities, 5, 27, 31, 54
Square as preferred shape, 11–13, 14
Steinhardt, Nancy Shatzman, 44, 45, 49, 50, 54, 86
Stockades, 25–26
Stone faced walls, 21–22, 81
Sui dynasty walled cities, 46, 48, 49, 50
Suzhou, Jiangsu, 10, 27, 32

Taigu, Shanxi, 33, 34, 88
Tainan, Taiwan, 25
Taipei, Taiwan, 24
Taiwan, 24–25
Taiyuan, Shanxi, 27, 87
Tamped earth walls, 2, 15–27, 46, 56, 90
Tang dynasty walled cities, 20, 38, 42–43, 45–49, 50, 51, 52, 77–78, 102
Tianjin, Hebei, 39
Tiananmen Gate, 66–68
Tiananmen Square, 71–74

UNESCO World Heritage Site, 89

Village walls, 24, 87

Wall-building traditions, 3–41
Wards (*fang*), 47
Water gates, 14, 28–29, 31–32
Wengcheng ('urn walls'), 31, 32, 64–65, 82, 83, 92, 93
Western and Chinese wall-building traditions compared, 7, 37–38

Xi'an, Shaanxi, 13, 42–52, 87
Xu Yinong, 10

Yuan dynasty walled cities, 43, 53–57

Zhaojiabao, Fujian, 24
Zhejiang, 14, 94
Zhongdu (Liao and Jin capital), 53, 102
Zhou period walled cities, 11–12, 16–17, 20, 35, 53